# All drawn by horseS

By the same author

ALL MADE BY HAND (John Baker)
THE COUNTRYMAN'S WORKSHOP (EP, Wakefield)
FARM WAGGONS AND CARTS (David & Charles)
FARM WAGGONS OF ENGLAND AND WALES (John Baker)
THE SHELL BOOK OF COUNTRY CRAFTS (John Baker)

# All drawn by horses

## James Arnold

**David & Charles**
Newton Abbot   London   North Pomfret (VT)

688.6
Ar64a

**British Library Cataloguing in Publication Data**

Arnold, James
    All drawn by horses
    1. Horse-drawn vehicles – Great Britain –
    History
    I. Title
    688.6          TS2010

    ISBN  0–7153–7682–9

First published 1979
Second impression 1985

Printed in Great Britain
by Redwood Burn Limited, Trowbridge, Wilts
for David & Charles (Publishers) Limited
Brunel House  Newton Abbot  Devon

Published in the United States of America
by David & Charles Inc
North Pomfret  Vermont 05053  USA

# Contents

Acknowledgements 6

Glossary 7

1 Historical Background 9

2 Coaches, Omnibuses, Trams, Hackney Cabs, Hotel Buses 17

3 Coachman- and Owner-Driven Carriages 35

4 Light Carts and Gigs 81

5 Goods Waggons and Drays 102

6 Tradesmen's Vans, Carts and Floats 123

Index 141

# Acknowledgements

I have pleasure in making acknowledgement of invaluable assistance and permission to use visual information to the following: R. C. Dobbs; Dodington Carriage Museum; J. G. Fowler; Edward Hart; Marie Hartley and Joan Ingleby; A. J. Kirby; Charles Martell; Gordon J. Offord; Oxford Railway Publishing Company/British Rail; Raphael Salaman; Science Museum, London; Messrs Thimbleby & Shorland, Reading; John Thompson; Gordon Winter; and David Wray. The source of information on which my illustrations are based is given in brackets at the end of the appropriate caption.

Readers who are engaged in making models are recommended to write to Oxford Railway Publishing Co, British Rail, Prints Dept, Dell Cottage, Bank, Lyndhurst, Hampshire, for lists of diagrams published by them. All diagrams are reductions from the standard scale of $1\frac{1}{2}$ inches to the foot and they give the fullest information. Most of them bear the stamp of the drawing-office together with the date. From the same source a very large selection of photographs is available at sizes convenient to the purchaser.

From the Science Museum, London, there is a considerable list of photographs of various types of passenger vehicle, likewise available in various sizes.

I would welcome comment and further information from readers.

JAMES ARNOLD
Rosedale
Newtown
Lower Eggleton
Ledbury
Herefordshire

# Glossary

**Barouche**   similar to landau but seating two; early Barouche had a groom or grooms, later without; coachman-driven

**Berlin**   closed coach, seating four on two perches; there was a very primitive carriage in the seventeenth century, but the design crystallised c1760

**Break**   originally for breaking horses to driving, 1831; developed into a carriage seating six or more facing, 1874. Breaks had coach-like box-seats and later came to be hired

**Britzska**   travelling carriage, seating two, convertible for sleeping, 1818; coachman-driven

**Brouette**   sedan, driven to one horse by running driver, 1668

**Brougham**   closed carriage, seating two, coachman-driven, 1838

**Brougham-waggonette**   late Brougham hybrid, with rear door

**Buggy**   light, hooded cart with hind-seat, on two wheels, 1773; American Buggy similar but on four wheels

**Cabriolet**   open carriage on two wheels, seating two, 1823; some Cabriolets ran on four wheels; owner-driven

**Caleche**   open carriage, seating two inside and two behind; coachman-driven

**Carriage**   although commonly meaning a vehicle, understood by coachbuilders to mean the underframe and wheels

**Chaise**   light, open, gig-like carriage, seating one or two, owner-driven, 1770; see **Post-chaise**

**Chariot**   closed coach, seating two, 1661; a **Post-chariot** was privately owned but driven by post-boys on hired horses

**Clarence**   a later Brougham, seating four, 1842; coachman-driven

**Coach**   generic term for closed four-seater; derived from the Magyar town Kocs, near Budapest where fine coaches were made

**Curricle**   light, open carriage, seating two, with groom behind, 1756; driven to two horses abreast, 1820; owner-driven

**Dennett gig**   designed by Bennett, 1920, named after actress(es)

**Diligence**   French stage-coach, often driven pickaxe by postilion

**Dog-cart**   originally to carry sporting-dogs, 1669; open, no hood, back-to-back seating for four; some ran on two wheels

**Dormeuse**   smaller version of Britzska, 1821

**Eridge Cart**   low-built cart, back-to-back seats, on four wheels, 1890

**Fourgon**   luggage carrier resembling a break, 1848

**Gig**   generic term for light, two-wheeled, one-horse carriage, seating two, 1791

**Governess Cart** or **Car**   low built on cranked axle, seating children under charge of governess; seats facing

**'Growler'**   a Hackney Carriage, often an old Brougham

**Hackney Carriage**   carriage for hire from stand in street; from French *haquenée*

**Hansom Cab**   Hackney Carriage originated by Hansom in 1834 and developed c1837 by Chapman

**Landau**   open carriage, from Germany 1743, developed 1860; coachman-driven; state landaus and carriages were driven postilion

7

**Landaulette-Brougham**  Brougham variant with folding head and self-acting steps

**Mail-coach**  to carry Royal Mails with passengers 1784; outside passengers from 1803; no seats facing the guard

**Manchester Cart**  Market Cart, seating four; first made in Manchester in 1870

**Norfolk Gig**  shooting gig to seat four back to back; driven to tandem or one horse

**Omnibus**  first ran in Paris in 1669 but was a failure; Lafitte introduced his omnibus in 1819, and Shillibeer's omnibus first ran in London in 1829

**Phaeton**  generic term for a variety of light carriages; originally seating two with grooms behind, evolved into many variations, some owner-driven.  Derives its name from Greek myth—Phaeton was the son of Helios, coachman to the Sun; when he sought to drive his father's team he lost control and fell through the clouds, nearly setting the world on fire

**Post-chaise**  similar to chariot but entirely hired; the early chaise was a light, two-wheeled gig

**Ralli-car**  light gig, 1898; some late Rallis on four wheels

**Sociable**  smaller landau, seating four, one hood, 1865

**Stage-coach**  began in 1640; carried outside passengers 1753

**Stanhope Gig**  hooded; designed for the Hon Fitzroy-Stanhope 1815

**Sulky**  very light single-seater, no body, 1800

**Tennis Cart**  medium-weight gig

**Tilbury**  early gig designed by Tilbury 1796; developed 1820 to tandem or one horse

**Victoria**  low-built, open carriage, without doors, seating two, 1860; coachman-driven

**Village Phaeton**  small Break with middle doors, 1890; hired

**Vis-à-vis**  two-seater state carriage, seats facing, 1768.

**Waggonette**  carriage seating six or more facing, 1842; had phaeton driving-seat and was privately owned. Both Waggonette and Break had top which could be removed. The Waggonette resembled station bus

**Whisky**  light gig, seating one on chair, 1769

**Whitechapel**  London Market Cart, back-to-back seating for four, 1842; driven to tandem or one horse.

NOTE: All definitions should be interpreted in the broad sense because of the variety in any one type.

# 1 Historical Background

When the heavy-draught horse had been bred, by crossing the knight's courser with the Black horse, the ox was gradually superseded in draught. However, the virtues and defects of both animals were to be tossed back and forth until the last days of animal draught.

For centuries much of the transport of goods involved the use of pack-horses, especially during the winter. Quite late in the eighteenth century and even in the early nineteenth century, there were large areas of upland Britain where transport by other means was impracticable. A pack-horse could carry from $2\frac{1}{4}$ to $2\frac{1}{2}$cwt in a pair of basket-panniers.

Apart from early four-wheelers, there were primitive two-wheeled carts which had disc-wheels and axles, joined in one unit and revolving between four stout pegs. (For further information, the reader is referred to *Old Yorkshire Dales* by Arthur Raistrick, Pan Books.)

In medieval and Tudor times, a great deal of the country's freight was carried on inland waterways. The larger rivers were being made navigable, so that inland towns situated on them had a direct link with the sea. The later development of the canal system greatly increased this method of inland communication.

Problems that were peculiar to road transport made their impact as early as the thirteenth century. Goods vehicles of that time had massive straked wheels, secured by protruding nails: in the City of London, for example, a by-law was passed in 1277 prohibiting such vehicles. After a long lapse, this law was reaffirmed in 1391. Nearly a century later, in 1485, there was a prohibition on all wheels with square-headed nails. It seems that the legislation of those times moved with even less speed than the vehicles it sought to control.

We have further evidence of heavy carriers being used to bring discarded timber from the shipyards as pay-loads rather than return empty. This was consequent upon the serious denudation of forest oak.

Definite reference to four-wheeled passenger carriers—known as 'long-waggons'—can be found in sixteenth-century documents. These vehicles carried as many as twenty-five persons, in varying degrees of discomfort. (Even the first-class passenger was a hardier being than his present-day counterpart.) The Acts favouring broad-wheeled waggons that were passed during the eighteenth century were met with opposition; much ingenuity being employed to overcome them.

It has been accepted that the first stage-coach ran in 1640. Riding in a coach with not very effective suspension, the intrepid traveller from London to Exeter could expect to reach his destination in about four days, barring the misadventures of the time. Notwithstanding the hazards of the notorious Salisbury Plain, the Exeter Road followed much of its present course and it must have been one of the best maintained of trunk routes. Even so, it was customary then, and for a long time after, for anyone having urgent business to proceed by boots and saddle, relying upon relays of post-horses.

By the mid-sixteenth century, there were fine coaches of German make, known as Pomeranians, slung on leather straps and light enough to be drawn on good roads by two horses. Elizabeth made her state progresses in a coach built by Boonen in 1560, though she preferred to travel on horseback riding side-saddle.

From *Packhorse, Waggon and Post* by J. Crofts (Routledge & Kegan Paul) we learn that the carriage of those times was 'commonly a large leathern box, hung upon chains and drawn by eight horses'. It was more unwieldy than the Pomeranian, and possibly provincial in origin. In the sixteenth century this type of carriage made the journey from Shrewsbury to London in eight or nine days. But such a leviathan must have been exceptional.

By the time of the Stuarts, a private coach had become a sort of status-symbol, so that considerable encouragement was given to the development and improvement of carriages. However, the condition of the roads outside a radius of thirty-five miles from London acted as a serious impediment to progress. *Packhorse, Waggon and Post* is a valuable source not only of information on this matter but also for the insight that it provides into the social environment of the period. We learn, for example, that a certain coach, built in 1633, had straked wheels carrying a total weight of 152lb of iron. Because the carriages of the sixteenth and seventeenth centuries left much to be desired in their riding, it was less fatiguing to travel on horseback.

During the later years attempts to improve their riding were made by introducing the Cee-spring for the lighter coaches and carriages, but the breakthrough had to await the invention of the elliptic spring in 1804. But until these developments occurred, the use of the strap-sling method meant that London coaches were normally loosely suspended for the city streets, but had to be tightly braced for travelling further afield over the poorly-surfaced roads.

By 1665, carriage windows were being fitted with glass lights. The most sought-after horses were Flanders mares, but on many country estates farm-horses were often used. Defoe, in his *Tour Through the Whole Island of Great Britain* (Dent), tells us that he had seen a lady drawn to a church near Lewes, in Sussex, by a team of six oxen. Over the whole country conditions and practices varied considerably, so that in regions like Devon and Cornwall there were people who rarely, if ever, saw a wheeled vehicle.

Hazards infinitely worse than highwaymen were encountered during the Civil War, when many a waggoner was left stranded because his team had been commandeered by either Royalist or Parliamentary troops. This hazard was partially met by running in 'broken convoy', whereby at least some of the waggons would escape, or by running at irregular times.

By the seventeenth century, the general condition of the main roads had so far deteriorated that even though water transport was used there were serious shortages of many essential goods, including domestic coal, the consumption of which had greatly increased. Because these conditions existed, the pack-horse continued for many more years, and in some regions was the sole form of transport. In such regions the traveller could proceed by horse along many miles of 'pack and prime' or causeway made part-hard and part-soft. In the south, many a traveller left the road to follow a way over adjacent land. On the better-maintained roads, heavy carriers were used by manufacturers sending large consignments of bulky goods, such as the maltsters of Hertfordshire and the clothiers of Wiltshire and Somerset. This form of transport was especially important for the clothiers as it provided better protection for the finished cloth than was possible when it was carried in the pannier of a pack-horse.

By the late eighteenth century, conditions were improving and over long distances the best stage-coaches were averaging 9–10 mph, though the mails were the most smartly timed. The carrier and stage-waggon, drawn by a team of six or eight horses, plodded their immemorial way at $2\frac{1}{2}$ or sometimes 3mph while the waggoners walked or rode at the head.

It was customary for those innkeepers, who were also postmasters, to supply horses for coaches and travellers, and considerable numbers of horses were kept at the major points on the trunk roads. The stage- and mail-coach services were very well maintained, with the guard ever ready to keep an eye on wayward drivers. Copeland, in *Roads and Their Traffic, 1750–1850* (David & Charles), gives a vast amount of information on maintenance, customs and misadventure, while Burke, in *Travel in England* (Batsford), gives a colourful and accurate account.

The slowness and inefficiency of long-distance goods carriage prompted Matthew Pickford, of Manchester, to introduce what he called 'Flying Waggons' in 1777, to run twice a week between Manchester and London. Each journey was to be performed in four-and-a-half days, and passengers would be carried as well as goods. By the early nineteenth century this service was operated with closed vans, mounted on elliptic springs and lighter wheels. The driver sat on a box-seat and there was a second seat behind for his assistant. The term 'fly' was applied to them in respect of their comparative swiftness of 4–5mph. A similar service on the canals introduced by Pickfords in 1820 used horses in stage-working.

During the later years of the eighteenth century, very many people were 'taking to the road' and there developed much local activity in the use of private carriages and gigs. It is from this period, that lasted until the end of the nineteenth century, that all the familiar types of two- and four-wheeled cart originated.

Although the advent and expansion of our railway system brought about the early demise of long-distance travel and transport by road, there nevertheless developed a great many feeder services to and from country stations during the remainder of the nineteenth century. An illustration of this may be found in the Directory for Herefordshire 1852, a region where the railways were comparatively late in developing: road passenger services were running as late as 1880; and there were innumerable short-distance carrier and horse omnibus services, using stations as rail-heads.

As with the present-day Motorail services, so in Victorian times private carriages could be conveyed on flat trucks which were attached to certain trains, while the families travelled in first-class carriages. This service enabled the Victorians to reach distant destinations far more quickly than was possible by road.

The eighteenth century was the formative period during which most of the features of carrier and coach design evolved. With later refinements the climactic stage was reached during the late nineteenth century. By that time, the manufacture of the many kinds of goods and tradesmen's vehicles was passing into the hands of the big firms that were equipped for quantity production. Only they could make economic use of expensive machines, such as hydraulic tyre-setters, introduced c1895 from America. These firms, like the railway workshops, worked from accurate scale drawings. If the 'father-to-son' tradition that had prevailed in the village workshops was absent from the large firms, the standard was still very high. Some of them made private carriages that were to be compared with the best. Many of them were catering for an export market that was a stimulus to change.

During the early part of the twentieth century, farmers often used vehicles that had been designed for purposes other than farming. These vehicles were bought second-hand after service as drays or Miller's Waggons; almost anything on four wheels was accepted. The carriers were little different from farm waggons, except in their greater size and the absence of ladders which could be made in the village. After the Great War there remained thousands of army drays, made at Woolwich and elsewhere, which were auctioned, to be bought by farmers who referred to them as 'government waggons'. They were clumsy affairs, but the new owners managed somehow.

Whenever the millers changed from horse to motor, they found a ready market for their waggons among farmers. The use of these vehicles, and the advent of the tractor, contributed to the end of the traditional farm waggon. The Miller's Waggon may be seen as the last of the traditional carriers. They survived until late in the nineteenth century—the Gloucester Railway Carriage and Wagon Company Limited were making them in 1897.

The finish of goods vehicles varied considerably according to the nature of the goods carried. At the bottom of the scale was the refuse cart, distantly related to the dung. cart. Coal carts, however, were very well designed. There was a curious uniformity about them, whether they had been made at Gloucester, Bristol, London or Beverley. They had large wheels, waist-beds and robust iron-work. In profile, they had a graceful sheer, rising sharply forward, with a deeply bowed front.

The carts and vans made for tradespeople and shopkeepers were gaily finished with plenty of publicity for their business. Most of the Spring-carts used by market gardeners were finished in bright colours with lining-out in a manner similar to that in use on narrow boats on the canals. All these vehicles had their wheels only slightly canted and dished. Many had van-type naves with patent oilaxles of either the Drabbles or the mail pattern. They were known as 'patent' to distinguish them from the older axles that were lubricated with grease.

Except for the Miller's Waggon, all those made for road-work had spring-mounted bodies from which the tongue-pole had been eliminated. In four-wheeled passenger carriages the perch, which was the equivalent of the tongue-pole, was generally retained after the advent of the elliptic spring, but was dispensed with in the landau. A glance through the 1898 catalogue issued by Laurie & Marner shows elliptic springs without perches but alternatively Cee-springs with perches. The great merit of the elliptic spring was that its resilience could be determined by the length and the number of leaves.

During the eighteenth century the problem of giving a good turning lock to the forecarriage hinged on the diameter of the fore-wheels. A diameter small enough to provide a satisfactory lock increased the draught of the vehicle; in contrast, a diameter large enough to provide a lighter draught only restricted the lock. With waggons the waist of the body was indented, or in the very late patterns smaller fore-wheels were fitted, which were at less of a disadvantage on good surfaced roads. With carriages, either the perch was dispensed with or, if Cee-springs were retained, the perch was contorted into a shape commonly termed a 'goose-neck' that allowed the fore-wheels to turn under.

There had always been arguments in the workshops, on the road and in Parliament about the relative merits of broad wheels and narrow wheels. Broad wheels were thought to smooth out the ruts, though they made extra work for the horses; narrow ones were always in trouble in the ruts though it was acknowledged that they were lighter in draught. At the same time it was realised that the greater the load the wider must be the tread. In the end, the problem was largely resolved by Telford and McAdam by the expedient of surveying roads with a minimum gradient of 1 in 30, where possible, and by finding out what the Romans did to make a smooth long-lasting surface. While Telford favoured a hard foundation, McAdam favoured a resilient one. When we see 40-ton 'artics' travelling in excess of 60mph we remember the 7-ton carrier travelling at $2\frac{1}{2}$mph.

Turnpike Trusts for the maintenance of the roads were being established all through the eighteenth century with the peak during the decades around the turn to the nineteenth, when the so-called Golden Age of Coaching was in being. Yet while the coaches bowled along our major roads there were still many roads where standards fell badly short. We do not know for how long the turnpike roads were effective between repairs but after the advent of the railways the diversion of traffic to the new form of transport produced a commensurate decrease in revenue from turnpike tolls, and the obvious consequence was a deterioration in maintenance. Short-term measures were of little avail and it was not until the county councils were established in 1888 and charged with responsibility that anything practical was done. This was the biggest event since the 'Broadwheel' Act of 1773, correctly known as The General Turnpike Act 13 Geo. III 1773. They not only made laws relating to vehicles, but established the erection of milestones along every main road and of guide-posts at every junction. No longer would it be necessary for the lone traveller to hire a guide of doubtful reliability. Many new roads were constructed to standard widths. The primary roads were made 99 feet wide between the hedges and the lesser ones 66 feet wide, the centre third of each being metalled, leaving a third to either side as grass verge. We may recognise such roads by their straightness and wide verges, even though the metalled centre has been widened at the expense of the verges. We are apt to forget that in those days, and right down to 1920, it was possible for the pedestrian and the equestrian to proceed along a public road in perfect safety and without constant apprehension.

Passing reference has been made to the conveyance of goods by water in earlier times. The products of the clothiers of Wiltshire and Somerset, together with bacon, cheese and other dairy products, were all conveyed along roads which converged on Lechlade, the highest navigable point of the Thames, and were then transported by barges to the London markets. It was cloth magnate Jack of Newbury's waggons, en route to Newbury, which had impeded the progress of James I. At Newbury the waggons discharged their loads on to the Kennet barges.

The early Trusts erected 'turnpikes' (swinging barriers) at each toll-house. This type of barrier was in use from 1695 until 1753 when gates were introduced. As is often the case the name that originally denoted one thing came by usage to have a different meaning. Thus the 'turnpike' came to mean the road itself.

It was in the face of customary official obstruction that the first mail-coach service was authorised by Pitt, going over the head of the Postmaster in 1794. From the first service, between London and Bristol, this extended rapidly and continued until it was transferred to the railways in 1841. The coaches were of four types, varying in tare weight, about 18cwt. The wheels had diameters of 42 inches fore and 54 hind, with treads of $1\frac{7}{8}$ inches, on a wheelbase of 78 inches and a track of $61\frac{1}{2}$ inches over treads.

As inaugurated they carried passengers inside, but from 1803 outside seating was provided for second-class passengers. Men usually travelled outside the coach, a custom that has continued down to the present time with men preferring to sit upstairs on double-decker buses. A mail-coach had no outside seat facing the guard. That place was occupied by the box for the guard's blunderbuss, etc. The mails had priority over all other traffic, and paid no tolls.

The making of coaches and private carriages, carts and gigs came largely to be concentrated in London where a number of the older-established firms had their premises in Long Acre. The business reputation and workmanship of the London makers at that time was so high that many of the provincial coachbuilders tended to follow their example, even advertising that they employed the 'best London workmen'. Long Acre was by no means long enough to accommodate all the firms, many of whom were to be found in neighbouring streets and even further afield. We should not presume from this that 'London made' vehicles were necessarily the best; many provincial builders set a very high standard. They and the best of the small country wheelwrights and coachbuilders were well-enough equipped with skilled men and tools to make and maintain the many types of passenger cart used in the provinces and the rural areas. They catered mainly for the country doctor, the parson and the farmer, who usually had little, if any, contact with London. Such a man would have no reason or inclination to make the journey to London to buy

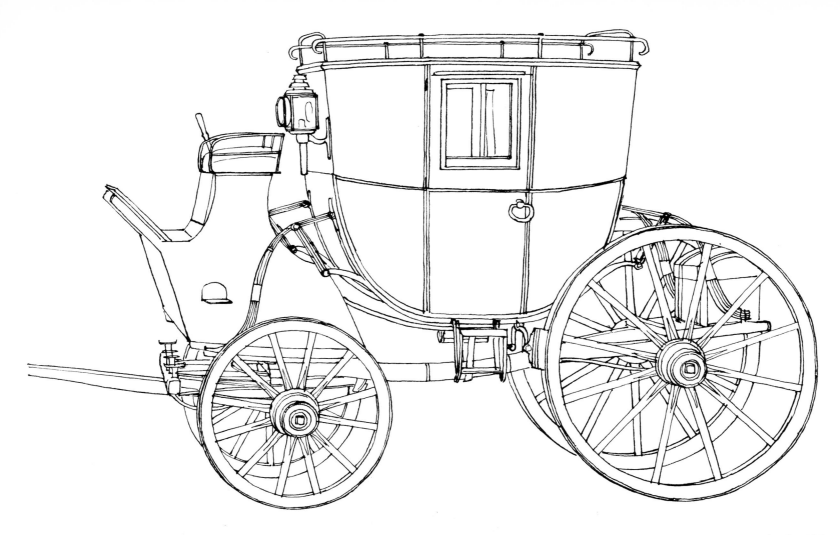

1 First mail-coach, London to Bath and Bristol, 1784

something that he could more conveniently obtain in his own locality. Country-type gigs like the Norfolk were indeed country-built.

The nineteenth-century doctor and parson were well aware of their social position which they maintained in the manner they thought proper. Some rode a horse of fine breeding, while others might drive a small Stanhope or even a landau. Such practices continued well into the present century, partly as a status-symbol, but largely because absolute reliability was essential. A doctor, making an emergency call during a cold night, could not afford to be delayed by a motor car whose engine was reluctant to function at that hour.

Very much depended upon the season of the year, the weather and the business concerned as to the means employed for making a journey. In the remoter hill country, doctor, parson, farmer, pedlar and postman made their rounds differing only in the type of vehicle, if any, employed, and the kind of horse. Where today the postman in central Wales delivers the mail by Land-Rover, his father (or grandfather) rode a sturdy pony. The pedlars and pack-men were a picturesque people, purveying news as well as goods, by cart or by pack-horse, according to their circumstances. Many a village publican ran a horse bus to the nearest railway station

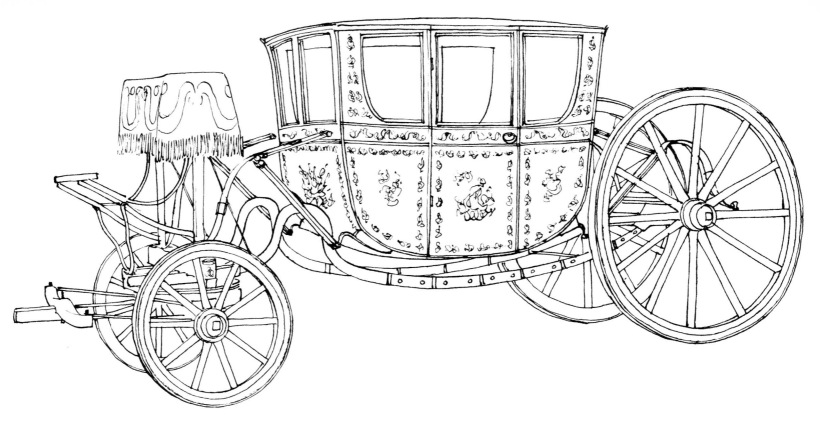

2   Berlin, built in France, *c*1780 (Suffolk Museum, Long Island, USA)

and from that beginning branched out into a thriving business.

It was during the nineteenth century that most of the types and patterns of the smaller passenger carts and gigs came into being and became established in the public mind. While town and park driving continued in the many varieties of landau and phaeton, the dog-cart, gig and waggonette were commonly used in the country.

The history of private coaches, carriages and gigs in the nineteenth century is, like the history of costume, a study of fashion, innovation and taste. We have noted, briefly, how the early vehicles, down to the eighteenth century, were both crude in the design of the undercarriage and uncomfortable in the body, and that the efforts of builders were concentrated largely on eliminating the defects of suspension. It was inevitable that as a result of various improvements, the earlier patterns or types of

carriage disappeared from the roads as new types arrived to establish themselves in public favour.

During the nineteenth century, then, some types of vehicle, such as the Berlin and the Caleche fell out of favour, giving place to the landau in all its variations. The landau has, indeed, proved one of the longest lived. Yet there were several types, such as the Barouche, that enjoyed favour for so long that as late as 1898 Laurie & Marner of Oxford Street, London, showed one in the catalogue commemorating their centenary. This elegant carriage retained the goose-necked perch and Cee-spring suspension. It was in effect a two-seater landau, which would explain its continuing popularity. As built by Laurie & Marner, it ran on wheels shod with rubber tyres. The solid rubber tyre was probably the most important advance after the invention of the elliptic spring.

Concurrently with the events concerning passenger carriages and carts during the nineteenth century, the larger wheelwrights and big coachbuilding firms were meeting the changing requirements of industry and the retail trade. An increasing variety of types

14

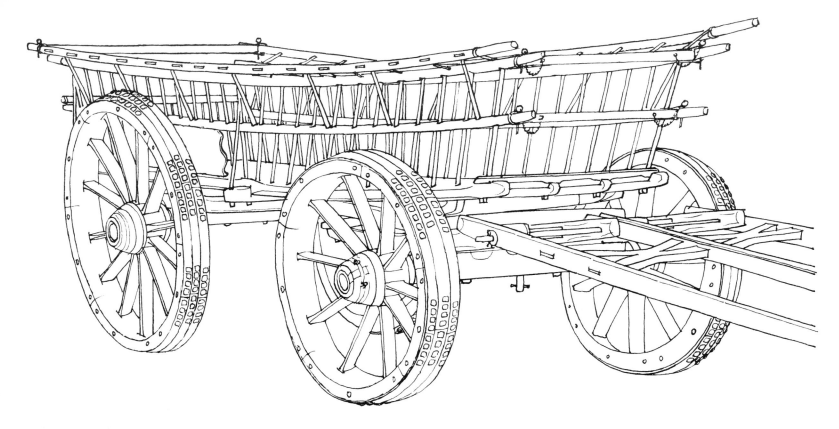

was produced, each type expressly intended for a particular purpose and designed to that end. Even tradesmen's and shopkeepers' closed vans and carts, however similar superficially, were differently arranged internally. It was significant that nearly all of the medium-weight vehicles ran on wheels built on mail patent axles, with the lightest of them running on Collinge axles.

The railways also had their own variety, some carriages being made by the big firms, some in the railway company's own workshop; the existence of this latter practice is not always recognised, but the workshops prepared designs and diagrams for every purpose and weight. These designs are available now from the joint venture of the Oxford Railway Publishing Company and British Rail.

The nineteenth century was the time of the station and hotel bus, that extremely attractive little vehicle that met people at the stations and conveyed them and their luggage to their final destinations. The two omnibuses were identical in design, with minor differences in detail and they were both with us to a surpris-

3 Road carrier, *c*1800, used in Sussex and Surrey (Science Museum, London)

ingly late date, especially in those rural districts where road services otherwise remained slight or uncertain, so that the small private omnibus became something of an institution. The driver knew everybody, and everybody knew him. He would wait at a stopping place for the older person who might not always get there on time and he was also a carrier of small parcels, which were dropped off at convenient points and, like the postman and the pedlar, he was a conveyor of news. It has been hinted that most tradesmen's vans were made by the large firms. While this was generally the case, it was not entirely so, because in any town, small or large, there were makers of all kinds of lighter vans and carts, who could offer the personal service that facilitated business.

We read and hear a great deal about the revival of the horse in riding and in draught. There is, of course, a sentimental overtone in this, but underlying the movement there is a growing realisation

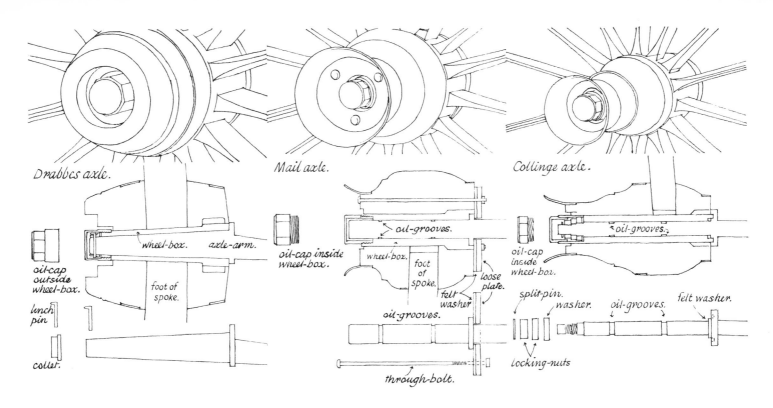

Drabbles axle.

Mail axle.

Collinge axle.

oil-cap outside wheel-box.

wheel-box. axle-arm.

foot of spoke.

linch pin

collet.

oil-cap inside wheel-box.

oil-grooves.

wheel-box.

foot of spoke.

felt washer

loose plate.

oil-grooves.

through-bolt.

oil-cap inside wheel-box.

oil-grooves.

split-pin.

washer.

oil-grooves.

felt washer.

locking-nuts

4 'Patent' axles: Drabbles, mail and Collinge axles

that on both road and land it is an economic necessity that a motive power be found that is both cheaper and, at the same time, more practical for certain purposes than the mechanically-propelled vehicle. The latter is increasingly found to be at a disadvantage in busy streets, so that it is beginning to defeat its own original purpose. Business prestige has precipitated a neck-and-neck race to own the largest vehicles, regardless of economics and practicability. A half-empty articulated lorry conceals, by its impressive impact, the fact that it is running at a loss. It does not conceal the fact that it is in everyone's way.

**Patent Axles**
Three types of axle were commonly fitted to the vehicles described in this book, all of them being lubricated with oil and therefore fitted with oil-retaining caps.

The heavier goods vehicles were usually fitted with Drabbles axles, which were tapered and had arms bolted to wooden axle-

beds, like farm-waggon axles. Drabbles axles were often fitted to the lately-built farm waggons.

The mail axles, so called because they were first fitted to mail-coaches, had parallel arms on 'through' axles, sometimes self-supporting, but often bolted to axle-beds. The naves were secured with three bolts to a loose, revolving collar with their nuts *behind* and could readily be detected by the heads of these bolts on the outer face of the nave.

A lighter type, called a Collinge axle, was patented by the designer in 1877. The nave, likewise running on a parallel axle, was secured by two lock-nuts and was commonly fitted to the lighter passenger vehicles, but it should be noted that many such vehicles were fitted with mail axles. These were made in at least eight sizes from 2 inches down to 1 inch, in graduations of $\frac{1}{8}$ inch. It appears that the decision as to the type of axle used rested with the builders.

The term 'patent axle', as used by the builders, unfortunately does not tell us what type of axle. The Collinge axle can be detected by the absence of the three bolt-heads *combined* with the smaller diameter at the nose of the nave.

# 2 Coaches, Omnibuses, Trams, Hackney Cabs, Hotel Buses

We are familiar with prints and pictures of scenes on the road and at the inns during the coaching age and also with photographs of preserved coaches being driven to shows. To the casual observer all coaches tend to look very much alike, but the presence or absence of identifying lettering will help us to distinguish between the mail- and stage-coaches and the Park Drags.

Apart from these differences and the arrangements of seating, these three types may be considered together, as the culmination of a long, slow process of technical development that had begun when the first stage-coach went on the road in 1640. The major step, that of suspension, had yet to be taken. This was dependent no less on the invention of the elliptic spring in 1804 than on a drastic change in road construction and maintenance. That there were some main roads in reasonable condition we may deduce from the run made by the first mail-coach between London and Bristol via Marlborough and Bath in 1784. Leaving London at 8 pm and Bristol at 4 pm the two runs were made in 16 hours.

The extension of the mail service to other parts of the country was made so rapidly that by 1791, the total daily mileage of all services was 6,896. A microcosm of the twenty-four hours over the whole country might be gained could we position ourselves at Hyde Park Corner, London, where we would see on average one coach passing every four-and-a-half minutes of the twenty-four hours, which means that at the peak periods of the day, the movement of coaches would be very heavy.

From every aspect it was a considerable step forward from the early coach—hardly more than an elaborate litter on wheels, drawn by horses. Such vehicles, then slung between supports on a long wheelbase, were cumbersome and heavy in draught. The German Pomeranian of the sixteenth century was good in its day for short journeys about London, but hardly suited to any long journey beyond the immediate radius of the capital. The normal capacity of a London coach was six persons, though two more could sometimes be carried—at a pinch. The passengers were protected from the elements by the leather curtains hanging at the windows, which effectively plunged the interior into gloom. The horses used were mostly Flanders mares, usually driven in teams of four, unless the road conditions demanded more, when the cock-horses were driven by postilion. Such coaches did well indeed to average twenty-five miles a day. Any distance appreciably in excess of this would have had adverse effects on both passengers and horses.

As an instance, the Cambridge coach of the seventeenth century took two days from London. The longest service at that time was from London to Newcastle. This was travelling 'first class' but we may visualise other travellers committing themselves to the conditions to be experienced on the travelling waggon. This vehicle carried several passengers cooped up in a hooded 'compartment' at the hind-end, the rest of the space being occupied by an infinite variety of goods and 'lesser' passengers. At some period intermedi-

5  Mail-coach (Science Museum, London)

ately between the seventeenth and eighteenth centuries, there were 'flying coaches' that covered the greater distances not so much by speed as by making a very early departure, at the cold hour of 2 am, and thence travelling for some twelve hours.

Contemporaneously with the stage-coaches one could, at greater expense, travel 'post', ie by chaise or hired coach, both being driven by postilions. Both the horses and the postilions or post-boys were hired from the innkeepers. The term post-boys may seem odd when applied to men who were often of advanced years.

Posting, although more expensive, was much quicker, but like the present-day car had its problems if the carriage was privately owned. People travelling by coach simply paid their fares in advance at the booking office, boarded the coach at the point of departure and got off at their destinations.

At this time in France the Diligence, a coach that carried no outside passengers, was in use. Being of 'two-and-a-half' compart-

18

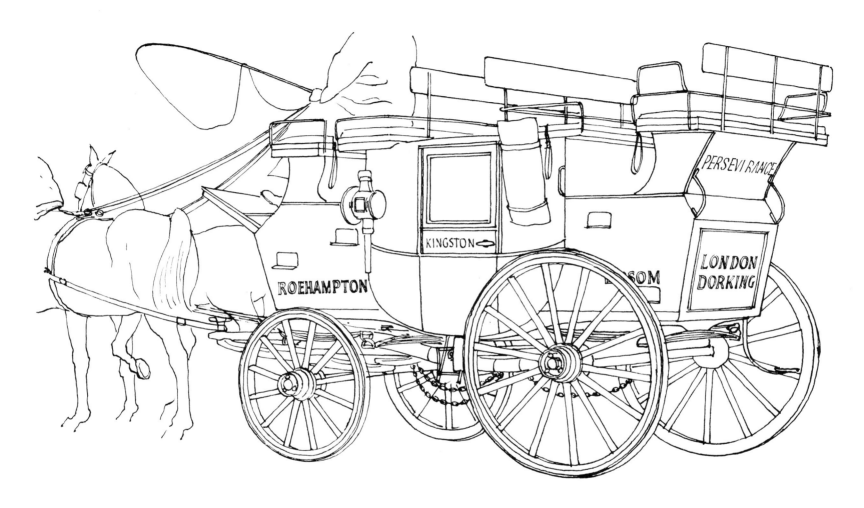

ments with the half compartment facing the horses, it was a larger and longer vehicle than the English coach. All the luggage was stowed on the roof, under a canvas sheet. (It is interesting to note that on the early railways, not only did the original carriage designs follow those of the road coaches but that luggage was stowed similarly and passengers below second class travelled much as did those in stage-waggons.)

The Diligence was usually drawn by four horses, but sometimes by five in pickaxe formation, that is with three abreast leading two

6  Stage-coach 'Perseverance' (Charles Martell)

wheelers, and in common with most continental coaches had a postilion on the left-hand horse ('near' to us but 'off' to France). A second man sat on a seat on the roof, presumably to control the leaders. According to visual references, the harness varied, some horses having the collar while others had the breast harness, with both types sometimes appearing in the one team.

If 'posting' was the most expensive way to travel, then the

stage-coach was the cheapest (excepting any means less satisfactory). In return for the faster but limited service provided by the mails, the fares charged were approximately double those charged on the stages, and while the mails were the smarter in their timing and operation, quick work at the inns with a stage-coach team could mean a change of horses in a minute or so and the coach would be away on its next run. Although the record for a change was 45 seconds, the usual time allowed, for everything, was five minutes, and a minute lost was a minute to be regained.

Conditions on the roads at the end of the eighteenth century varied from the fairly good to the impossible. The run of severe winters experienced at that period resulted in havoc on many roads that had been undermined by flood water, or where bridges had been washed away or damaged. At that time and until the creation of the county councils, road construction and maintenance depended upon the Statute of Labour and the material available in the vicinity. This meant, for example, that the main roads in the Home Counties were among the worst in the country, whereas those in regions where good stone was readily available were among the best.

The expenses of coach operation consisted of maintenance of coaches, hiring charges and the wages of coachmen, guards and stable-boys, turnpike tolls and the duty and licences levied by the government, which were based upon seating capacity. A driver averaged about fifty miles per day, going out and returning, so that anyone travelling a considerable distance met a number of drivers and guards. With a fully-laden coach one may wonder where the centre of gravity lay, and reckless driving in an effort to regain lost time or to compete with other coaches could and did result in some alarming accidents.

The firms operating the stage-coaches varied greatly in size from the very large ones, keeping more than 1,000 horses and 50 coaches, down to the innkeeper who had a 'share' in a coach and who agreed to supply the horses. From a variety of sources it is clear that the horses used in coaching operations were supplied in several ways: by innkeepers, by the operators themselves and by jobmasters who specialised in the supply of horses for every class of operator. In contrast to the hard-pressed jobmaster, the small operator with a few horses was easily accessible in the small towns and villages.

On every coach, the guard was senior to the driver and had to make any decisions arising on the journey. On mail-coaches the guards were totally responsible for the mail that was carried and were forbidden to collect or deliver letters en route, so preventing any interference with the consignment. They had to ensure that the number of passengers being carried did not exceed the number allowed.

Outside passengers, paying second-class fares, were carried on the stage-coach from 1753 and on the mails from 1803. The guard on a mail-coach was armed with a blunderbuss and pistol, which were carried in a box in front of him on the roof. No seating was provided facing the guard. He also carried a regulation time-piece, a reminder that until 'railway time' was instituted throughout the country, time was regulated according to the sun with the result that times varied all over the country. The guards of both mail- and stage-coaches carried a long horn, kept in a wicker container on the near side of the coach. They used this horn to give warning of the coach's approach to the keepers of the toll-gates that had to be opened in advance for the mails, for which no toll was charged. The tolls for the stages, especially the less patronised ones, were the cause of many complaints by the operators. The horn officially supplied to the mails guards was made of tin and did not produce a particularly satisfying note. Many guards therefore provided themselves with horns made of copper or brass, which gave a far more melodious tone.

With reference to the seating, the mails had a single seat each for driver and guard, whereas the stages could accommodate passengers side by side with drivers and guards in addition to those facing the guard. A glance at any of these coaches will enable us to understand why Englishmen preferred to travel 'outside'. At a second-class fare, he had a first-class position from which to enjoy the passing scene (except in adverse weather).

The horses used on the coaches were usually Yorkshire Coach or Cleveland, but in fact they appear to have varied from the well bred, well trained and well cared for to 'the blind and the halt'. The day services were the best equipped although some of the teams on the middle stages were of doubtful quality. In this respect, the night services were the least satisfactory. Efficient running of the service depended upon the teams containing four well matched horses, for one 'rogue' would upset the other three when something untoward occurred. The off leader was very often a white or grey for visibility at night. The horse's working life seems to have been about four years on the best, fast services, but on the quieter, cross-country ones, the working life was probably seven years after which a broken horse found its sad way to the knacker's yard or the shafts of a rural station fly.

The infinite care that is bestowed upon horses today by people and societies engaged in their preservation should not blind us to the many abuses that did occur in times past. A drunken driver

7 Park Drag (Science Museum, London)

was bad enough, yet even with care and consideration accidents could and did happen from a variety of causes, ranging from traffic and weather to human error.

The advent and rapid growth of the railways certainly brought about the demise of goods and passenger transport by road, but the end did not come about within a few years, but gradually, as each group of services was displaced by a new line of railway. Many operators fought hard in a battle they were slowly losing, resorting to various measures that could only be of short duration. In regions where the railways were slow in developing or where the lines were less penetrating, many coach services continued, often linking up with mainline stations. These localised services continued until as late as 1880 and some of the roads in these 'underdeveloped' areas carried a fairly heavy volume of traffic.

After the 1840s many coaches found new owners in whose hands they came to be known as Park Drags (illus 7). A drag may be defined as a kind of vehicle similar to a stage-coach, with seating inside and out, but one in private ownership. As they were not public service vehicles, we find little reference to them in literature until the present time. Their definition in the *Oxford English Dictionary* gives the date 1755 which can only mean that such vehicles were in use during the second half of the eighteenth

21

8 Road coach, by Holland & Holland, 1875 (Suffolk Museum, Long Island, USA)

century, and this in turn implies that these vehicles were either constructed for their owners to resemble stage-coaches or were purchased second-hand from stage-coach operators. Later they became common, especially at race meetings, because their owners could use them as private grandstands. Originally, the drags were coachman-driven and it is only in comparatively recent years that many enthusiasts have cultivated the fine and by no means easy art of handling four well bred horses.

Driving a coach along a level road in fine weather is the rosy picture of coach travel, but the services were maintained as well as circumstances allowed in almost every kind of adverse weather.

Such weather conditions were recorded by artists whose pictures are available today in the form of reproductions. The run of bad winters that occurred between 1790 and 1830 has already been mentioned and a valuable picture of the climatic conditions prevailing at this time can be found in books concerning the agriculture of the period.

Services that ran over very hilly country provided ample opportunities for the exercise of the driver's skill in the proper use of the brakes and control of the teams. Motorists who now traverse the 'old coach road' between Devil's Bridge and Rhayader in Wales in a matter of minutes might well pause at the top of the last descent and imagine themselves in charge of a four-in-hand. No team could hold a coach on such a descent without the use of the brakes and drug-shoe.

22

Two kinds of brake were fitted to every coach—the shoe acting on the hind-wheel rims, operated by either a pedal or a very long right-hand lever, both through rods and cranks. The lever was useful not only when stationary but as an auxiliary to relieve the driver's foot. The drug-shoe was an additional device, a cast-iron U-sectioned block on a long chain, which when not in use hung on a hook on the near-side frame close to the hind-wheel. At the top of the hill, the driver stopped the coach and the guard jumped down and placed the drug just in front of the point where the near wheel met the ground. The chain was of such a length that when run taut it lay exactly under the wheel to carry it stationary down the hill. On a long descent the shoe could become very hot! At the foot of the hill the coach was backed a yard or so and the guard replaced the drug on its hook and the coach then continued its journey. The roller-scotch used on waggons was not fitted to coaches.

The body of a coach consisted of a framework of ash, panelled with sheets of deal, covered with leather with all joints and edges sealed by beading, but the bodies of later coaches were painted and varnished. The floor was mahogany, covered with oil-cloth and fitted with a carpet. The windows were framed in mahogany and could be raised or lowered by means of a leather strap. The inside walls were lined with drab lace and the cushions were stuffed with horse-hair. For the convenience of passengers there was a pocket on the inside of each of the doors. As in the first-class railway carriages there were loop-leathers hanging on each side of the doors. There was no form of interior lighting. The whole body was built on an oak underframe, extending the full length and width of the coach. Access on either side was by means of iron steps that were folded up when not in use.

The outside seats overhung the roof by about 10 inches on each side. The seat for the driver and a passenger was supported on brackets above the front boot, the floor of which could be opened to allow luggage to be stowed. (Luggage could also be accommodated in the hind boot.) The guard's seat was similarly supported. The driver's seat was inclined slightly for better driving (this incline was common to nearly all carriages). The driver's foot-board projected well forward from the body of the coach. On the splinter-bar and on the boot sides there was a series of steps for access to the outside seats. On the fore-corners of the body there were brackets to take the coach lamps. These lamps were usually square but on some coaches they were barrel shaped. The lighting was by means of candle or sperm-oil, the candle being spring-loaded so that as it burned, it was pushed up the tube. Behind the candle or wick there was a silvered glass; there was a convex glass on the front and a plain one on the outer side. On the hind-corner of the body there was a basket holder for the coachman's horn and on some of the drags there was a similar container for umbrellas.

Mail-coach drivers wore a grey multi-caped coat, while the guards were resplendent in scarlet coat and jack-boots. They had to keep a watchful eye on any wayward driver who might be less imbued with pride in the job. Years later, when the coaches were running for the last time, many a guard found a similar job on the railway, for which he was well suited. The drivers probably found their way to the seats of the road vehicles used by the railways.

The tongue-pole of the carrier had its equivalent in the perch of the coaches, and the sway-bar or slider on the forecarriage was likewise retained though the whole forecarriage was differently constructed. Hounds were replaced by short futchels that secured the extremities of the splinter-bar. Although the through axle was an early adoption, the wooden axle-bed was retained on all heavy coaches. The perch, when viewed in side-elevation, had a definite 'sag' between the fore- and hind-axles, to clear the lowest part of the body. The draught-pole was detachable and fitted into brackets, where it was pinned rigidly in place. On the fore-extremity there was a large hook, so designed that the eye of the swingle-tree could be disengaged. This hook was called a crab. Coach undercarriages had either semi-elliptic or 'telegraph' springs.

The stocks, spokes and fellows of the wheels were made of elm, oak and ash respectively. With their more slender dimensions, there was a need for and room for more spokes, which were set staggered round the stock. There were 12 spokes in a fore-wheel and 14 in a hind-wheel with only a slight dish and cant. The fore-wheels had diameters of 42–45 inches and the hind-wheels had diameters of 54–57 inches with treads of $1\frac{7}{8}$ inches. The wheels ran on mail axles with a track of 60–62 inches over the treads and a wheelbase of 78–80 inches. The average tare weight was 18cwt.

The mail axle was not to be confused with the Collinge axle. Both had parallel arms but the Collinge was secured by two lock nuts and a washer, the mail had three bolts right through the stock from a back plate to the front circular plate. The back plate rotated freely on the axle-shoulder while the front was clear. Mail patent axles were eventually fitted to many types of vehicle and became available to builders in eight diameters from 1 to 2 inches.

According to a diagram prepared by David Wray of a mail-coach c1820–30, the axles were then still lubricated with grease, which suggests that oil lubrication came into use rather later. The container-cap had an octagon nut on the periphery for the spanner and all caps had a right-hand thread for near and off axles and

9   A typical 'growler' (Science Museum, London)

screwed to the inside of the wheel-box. The face of the cap was usually inscribed with the builder's name but very often with that of the owner; only on farm waggons did they always carry the wheelwright's name.

The mail axle can immediately be detected by the three nuts on the outer face, and the fitment was not confined to coaches. The Gloucester Railway Carriage and Wagon Company fitted certain of their vehicles with this type, including omnibuses, carriers and large Breaks and waggonettes, and even used it on some of the lighter carriages.

Bearing in mind that hooped tyres were made during the Iron Age, anywhere between Asia Minor and Britain, it comes as a surprise to read that a man named Hunt is reputed to have invented the tyre in 1767. It has, of course, occurred in history that ideas have been lost and then rediscovered at a later date. When the Romans departed from this country, the native Celts were gradually pushed back by the Saxons, who in turn received similar treatment first from the Danes and then from the Normans, and during these years the roads built by the Romans suffered from disuse and neglect except on the big estates. Consequently when wheeled vehicles later increased in number they had to be used on roads that were quite unsuitable for them.

In the tussle between the supporters of broad wheels and their opponents who favoured narrow wheels, it was inevitable that some wheelwright should rediscover the hooped tyre. It is likely that after 1767 the tyre received its strongest support from the makers and operators of the coaches.

Proper maintenance kept breakdowns to a minimum. However, with the prescribed kit of tools most breakdowns on the road, short of such disasters as a broken wheel, could be dealt with on the spot. The full kit of a mail-coach contained a hammer, a wrench and spanners, etc, together with lengths of various chain and shut-links and an assortment of small parts. In addition to all this, the operators had to ensure that the horses were well shod, wherever this was not the responsibility of either the innkeepers or the jobmasters. With the onset of winter all shoes had to be prepared for the weather conditions likely to be encountered.

The stage-coaches acquired self-advertising liveries by displaying the names of the places each coach served. The idea adopted by the railways of destination boards was never used by coach operators, so that all place names were lettered permanently on the body-sides. This meant that any one coach always worked on the same route, and a name, such as Regulator or Comet, was often associated with that route.

The mail-coaches were more soberly treated, without advertise-ment, and had a uniform livery in the excellent taste of their age. Although some coaches had all black liveries, the majority had maroon and black with scarlet undercarriage, wheels and poles. All scarlet parts were lined out in black, all maroon parts were lined out in gilt. The destinations and the words 'Royal Mail' were in gilt, the destinations being above the waist and 'Royal Mail' on the door panel above and below the royal arms. On some coaches the destinations were set in two lines and on others in one line, any one place leading on one side of the coach and following on the other side. The style of lettering was either bold serif or sans serif.

The initials of the monarch were in italic scroll on the fore near and off sides and the coach number on the hind near and off sides. On the top quarters to either side of the door the badges of four Orders were displayed in this sequence: fore near, Order of the Garter; fore off, Order of the Bath; hind near, Order of the Thistle; hind off, Order of St Patrick. With the solitary exception of one mail-coach named Quick-silver, none of them bore a name.

The history of urban passenger transport affords an interesting study of the transition from one means to another, as various types of conveyance appeared on the streets, went through their 'life-span', and suffered gradual elimination by a successor that was tried and proved or disproved. In the London of the later nineteenth century there were three types of passenger transport; the horse-drawn omnibus, the Hackney Cab or 'growler', and the Hansom Cab.

Carriages for hire, called Hackney Coaches in their day (illus 9), appeared as early as 1605. They held a monopoly in business until the advent of the Cabriolet in 1823. The Cabriolet was originally designed to be a coachman-driven town carriage for two persons. It had two wheels and was drawn by one horse. There were later versions running on four wheels.

With the rapid increase in traffic, the existing congestion was much aggravated and the sedan chair had the advantage of greater mobility. It had found its place during the eighteenth century and it was during the nineteenth century that it acquired a pair of wheels with one man drawing the handles. The sedan now travelled at a run instead of a walk. However, the era of the sedan had ended by the middle of the century when the last stand, in St James's, was closed.

The later 'coaches' could be any vehicles that were suitable. Eventually, with the passing of the decades, many of the Hackneys could be identified as being down-graded from a higher status. Many a Brougham or Clarence found its devious way to a cab-stand. The term 'cab' suggests a common origin in Cabriolet, but

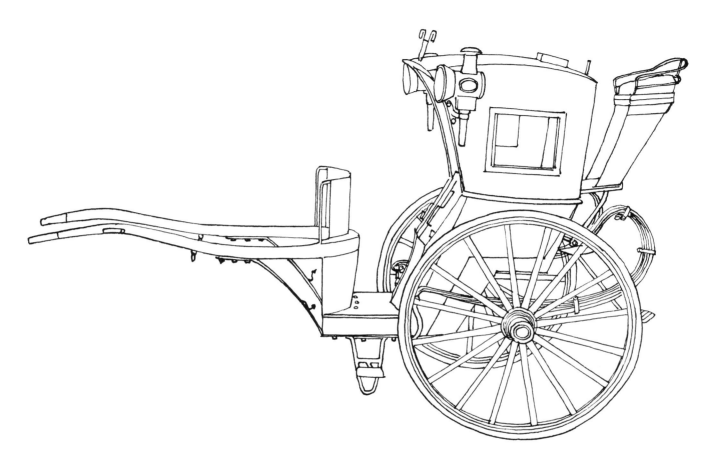

10   Hansom Cab (Science Museum, London)

the exception to this was the Hansom Cab, which was specifically designed for the purpose for which it was employed. It takes its name from Joseph Hansom, who designed a carriage in 1834. The characteristic features (familiar to most of us through pictures), with the driver seated high behind the semi-open-fronted compartment, were not present until the 'Hansom' appeared on the streets in the modified form designed by John Chapman (illus 10). He called his design a Hansom Cab, although the originator had no connection with this later type.

We have long been familiar with an important essential difference between public service vehicles in Britain and those on the Continent. With a few exceptions in certain cities, such as Berlin, buses and trams on the Continent have always had 'inside' (ie, lower deck) accommodation only and this applied also to the French Diligence. Paradoxically, double-deck passenger trains on suburban services are not uncommon on the Continent. The early adoption of seating outside or 'on top' in Britain influenced the design first of coaches, then of omnibuses and finally of trams. Indeed, the practice is so ingrained that single-deck vehicles have only been used where the passenger traffic has not warranted the double-decker.

The early double-deck omnibus had only a vertical ladder for access to the 'top deck' and a short time elapsed before a more convenient access was evolved in the spiral steps that turned a

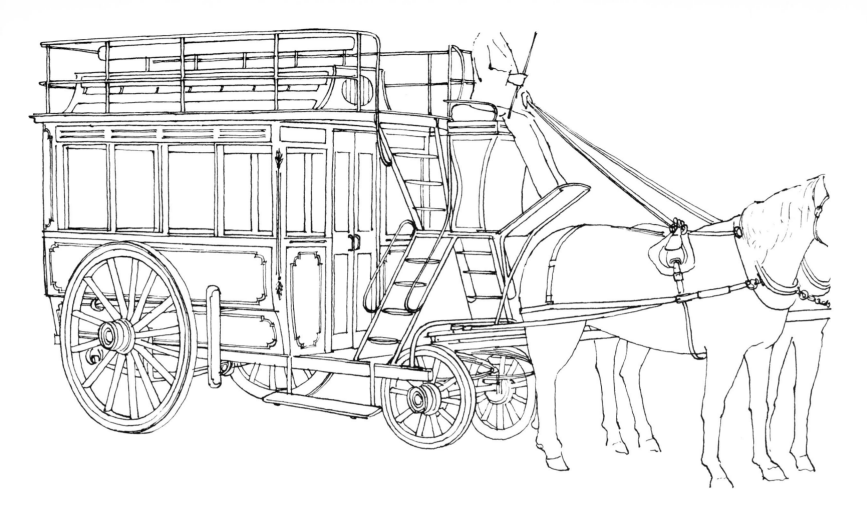

quarter circle from the platform. It may be remarked that in 1905 the London United trams, built in Lancashire, developed the steps further with a dog-leg stair that had a landing half way.

During later years when the horse-drawn omnibus was ubiquitous in every town and city, the electric tram was becoming a status-symbol of progressive administration and business—the phrase 'electric trams pass the door' was an advertising slogan that indicated a flourishing business, and the opening ceremony of the first tram route in any town was an affair of pomp and circumstance attended by every dignitary. A transition between the omnibus, which did not run in tracks, and the electric tram, was provided by the horse-drawn tram.

In an era of apparent permanency, where the speed of traffic

11  'Knifeboard' omnibus, c1881 (Science Museum, London)

was determined by the horse, the tram was a milestone in the evolution of passenger transport. Structurally it had its origin in the omnibus, but differed from that vehicle in having access to both decks at each end. The access that was used depended upon the direction in which the tram was travelling.

At this point it is of immediate interest to know what loads a draught horse can pull. The pack-horse (which was never a heavy horse) could carry nearly three hundredweight, distributed in two panniers. On a water-bound flint road in good condition, the heavy horse could draw at least one ton, and on a railway track it could draw up to ten tons. The maximum load that could be drawn by

12   London General Omnibus Company pair-horse omnibus, c1910
(Science Museum, London)

a horse was seventy tons. This load would be carried on a horse-drawn barge on a canal or navigation.

So we come now to what the horses were required to do in urban transport, where the frequent starting and stopping must have told considerably. They were more fallible than motors and the psychological element played some part, especially in adverse conditions. With good, sympathetic drivers, who understood their horses, a high performance could be obtained, but if the driver was less competent and at all ill-tempered then the horse's performance inevitably suffered. This element of sympathy between the driver and his horse has always been vital and is a major factor in any return to draught by horse.

A double-deck omnibus, at the turn of the century, carried 28 passengers and had a laden weight of 2½ tons. Each horse omnibus required a string of eleven horses, working in pairs in rotation with the fifth day spent at rest. Each pair was on every run in service with the eleventh horse as a spare.

The horses had a working life of some four years, or five in the best circumstances. While single-deck omnibuses working an easy route could be drawn by one horse, two were always used on the double-deck omnibuses, and where conditions were difficult, as on some hilly routes, it was usual to have three horses abreast. Omnibuses used on these routes had twin draught-poles, with the middle horse between them. All three horses had pole-harness, and the horses generally chosen were of a cross-bred draught, fairly clean about the legs. A typical tram drawn by two horses weighed about 5 or 5½ tons laden. Some part of the advantage of the rail over the road was thus lost by the much heavier vehicle.

All the early omnibuses carried the 'inside' passengers facing across on seats set lengthwise, a design practice that was continued well into the motor era. The London General Omnibus Company's B class, or B Generals, as we knew them then, were the last London omnibuses to have this style of seating. It was on the next type, the K, that cross-seating was introduced.

A similar style of seating arrangement was used on electric trams. On the top deck both omnibuses and trams had cross-seats, although on the original omnibuses lengthwise seats facing outward—generally known as 'knifeboards'—had been introduced in 1851 (illus 11). When the cross-seats were introduced on omnibuses in 1881 they quickly became known as 'garden seats' (illus 12). The aisle between the rows was not central but one-sided, with single seats on one side and double on the other.

I was a schoolboy when the B Generals were still running, during the early 1920s, and I must say that I found that they had a disconcerting sway on any curve at the foot of a hill. I didn't like them at all, but I imagine that the Edwardian passengers saw things differently. Their top decks overhung the lower much as the jettied floors of timber-framed houses overhang the lower ones, making them appear distinctly top-heavy. This top-heaviness was offset only by the weight of the complete chassis.

Since only the most daring of ladies ever intruded into the male domain outside on the stage- and mail-coaches, it became something of a national custom that the top deck of an omnibus, whether horse-drawn or motor-propelled, was exclusively for male passengers, even though the means of ascent and descent underwent considerable improvement over the years.

Many people are aware that George Shillibeer ran the first London omnibus in 1829. He had built omnibuses in Paris and returning to London had set about the matter of providing a service in that city. He called his vehicle an 'omnibus' from the word devised by the Parisian operator, Lafitte, in 1819. In Paris, the omnibus had been preceded by vehicles carrying no more than eight passengers; these had not been a success. Shillibeer's first omnibuses carried twenty-two passengers and were drawn by three horses abreast. Somehow they look distinctly European rather than British.

In the heyday of the London horse omnibus, the streets were indeed colourful. The present-day idea of uniformity was something then unheard of, and lay in the future beyond the war that was yet to come. The omnibuses were painted in a variety of colours: reds, blues, yellows, greens and purples, each colour assigned to a particular route. This made it easier to identify the vehicles on each route. The obverse side of the London Transport coin was the elimination of diversity so that eventually all buses and trams were *red* with the brown lower panel eliminated and the white changed first to grey, and then to cream and reduced in total area. When London United Tramways began, in 1905, the trams running from Shepherd's Bush to Southall were all white, those to Hounslow were red and white, while those running to Hampton Court were blue and white. The blue trams retained their livery long after the all-white had gone red.

In contrast to the florid display on the London omnibuses, some of the provincial types show a fine restraint. In an official photograph taken by the Gloucester Railway Carriage and Wagon Company of an omnibus made by them for the Glasgow Tramway and Omnibus Company in May 1894 every detail is shown clearly. The design (illus 13) shows a considerable advance on contemporary London omnibuses and is very restrained in its livery, with no lettering except the two destinations. Presumably designed for a hilly route, it was equipped with twin draught-poles for three

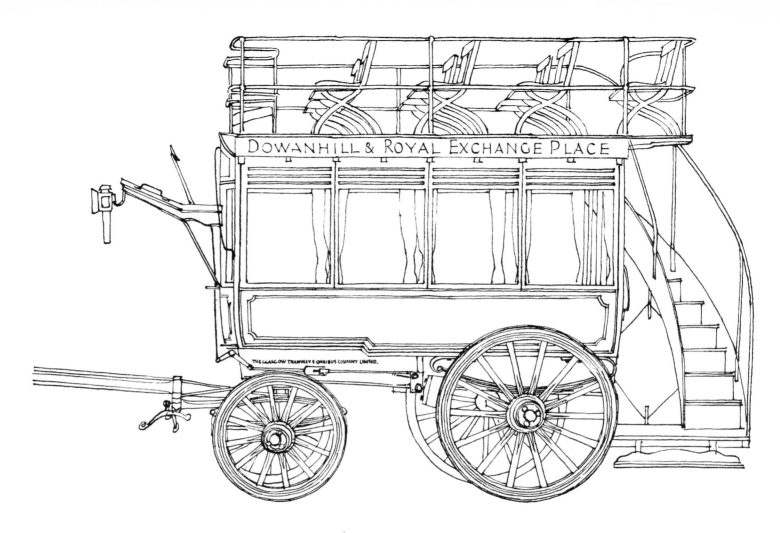

13 Glasgow three-horse omnibus, by Gloucester Railway Carriage and Wagon, 1894 (Oxford Railway Publishing Co/British Rail)

horses abreast. Access to the top deck was by means of the partially-enclosed spiral staircase, but the top deck, curiously, was wholly open with stanchions and rails like those on a ship. Note the gently sloping floor and the single large headlamp on the driver's footboard. This design of omnibus ran on mail axles. A nice feature of the inside fittings was the curtains that could be drawn across the windows.

The spiral step or stair access to the top deck was introduced during the decade 1860–70. Necessity was obviously the mother of invention. Some years were to pass before the introduction of the 'garden seats'. On both types of omnibus the driver's position was a little above the roof but below the passengers, several of whom could seat themselves either side of the driver (this was not possible on the Glasgow type because of the railings). As with all heavy-draught vehicles the drivers sat well above the horses.

The harness used was simpler than that used on most heavy-draught waggons and carts. There was no back band, no breeching and no ornamental straps, only the normal collar. All braking was done by the pedal-operated shoes on the hind-wheels.

The 'garden-seat' omnibuses were rather larger than those which had a 'knifeboard' seating arrangement and carried more

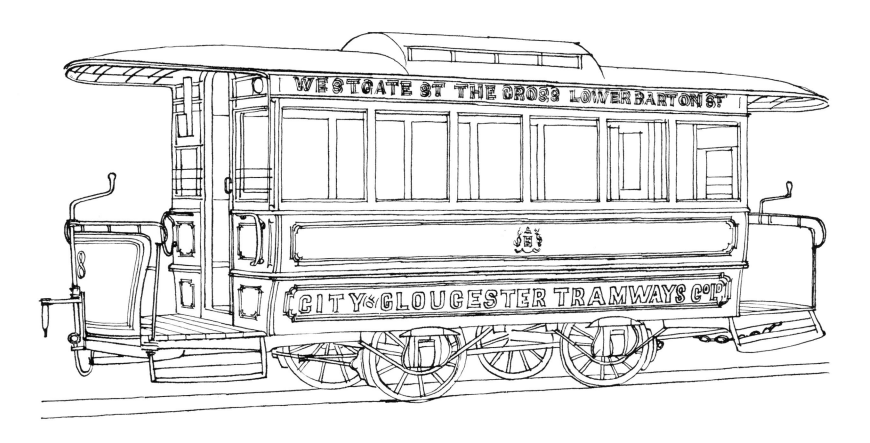

WESTGATE ST THE CROSS LOWER BARTON ST

CITY & GLOUCESTER TRAMWAYS Cᵒ ᴸᵀᴰ

passengers. The bodies of the former had four windows on each side against three a side on the knifeboards.

As an example of the design of the horse tram let us look at a new type of single-deck vehicle introduced in 1886 by the City of Gloucester Tramway Company (illus 14). It was built in the city by Gloucester Railway Carriage and Wagon Company. Like the Glasgow bus of eight years later, it was no laggard in design and incorporated most of the features of the later electric trams. It had six good windows on each side and a partially clerestoried roof. It was controlled by the driver with a screw-on brake and was light enough to be drawn by one horse.

The small buses used by hotels and for serving country stations

14 Gloucester tram, by Gloucester Railway Carriage and Wagon (Charles Martell)

had a low box-seat for the driver and a light forecarriage with shafts (illus 15). Such a vehicle could accommodate four people or six at the most, with access at the hind-end. The roof was railed all round to contain the luggage. Such vehicles were used everywhere in the country and most of the more important hotels in the country districts had at least one of these handsome little carriages.

In 1884, the Stratford works of the Great Eastern Railway prepared a diagram for a proposed one-horse omnibus. It was essentially similar in design and layout to the small station and

15  Pair-horse hotel omnibus (Science Museum, London)

hotel omnibuses that were very common, until the motor bus and car took their place.

The body of the Great Eastern bus was 66½ inches long and 62 inches wide and the distance from the front to the fore-axle centre was 16 inches. With a wheelbase of 67 inches, the fore-wheels had a diameter of 50 inches and the hind-wheels had a diameter of 64 inches. The spoking was 12 in fore and 14 behind. The diagram does not show the type of patent axle, but it is most likely that this was the mail type. The driving-seat, of the box type, was similar to that on a waggonette or coachman-driven carriage, as were the driving-seats of all station buses, and was inclined.

The body had an arc-roof of a radius common to small buses, that is, deeper than on private carriages. The interior was appointed to much the same standard of comfort as a first-class railway carriage, with ample windows, ventilators and blinds and a rack for light articles. All other fittings, such as lever-brake,

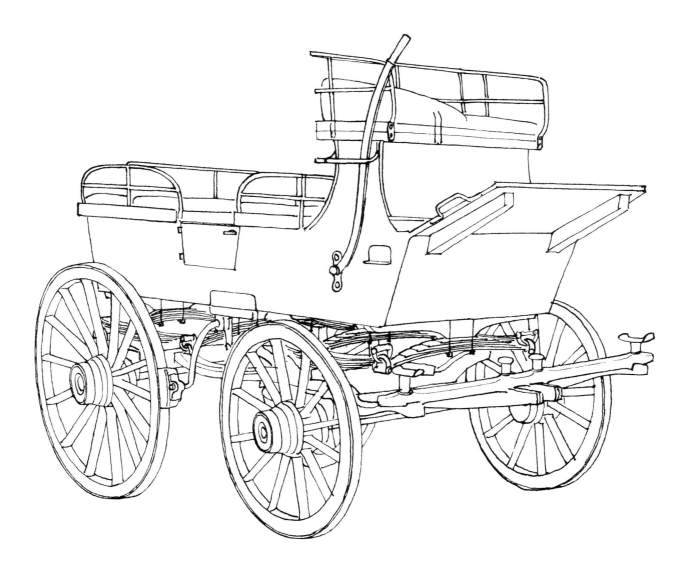

lamps and roof-rack were standard. This bus seated four people, though some could seat six. It is worth noting that many private waggonettes were built to be convertible, with a removable top half like that of a bus. In the coach-house, in which the waggonette was stored, there was a hook and rope on a pulley which was used in order to remove or replace the top. In comparison with our frenetic lifestyle, life, at least before 1910 and certainly before 1900, was comparatively leisurely with the speed of the horse determining the pace of everything on the road and the farm.

Even until World War II the buses were restricted to 12mph.

The Charabanc (illus 16) was another derivative of the large Break and first arrived in this country as a present for Queen Victoria. From this beginning it evolved into a fairly heavy vehicle with cross-seats which could be entered from either side. Doors were added at a later date when the Charabanc became mechanised. As this was essentially a carriage for large party

17 Wagonette in Wharfedale, Yorkshire, c1910 (Marie Hartley and Joan Ingleby)

outings, each row of seats was a little higher than the row in front, making the hind row an appreciable height from the ground. Access to all seats was by means of a step-ladder, carried on the vehicle. The driver had his place in the centre of the front row. The undercarriage was robustly constructed but had no perch and the through axles were not supported by axle-beds. The wheels were much more robust than those of the early coaches and had mail axles. Two horses were harnessed to the draught-pole. The early Charabanc showed distinct evidence in its body of its derivation from the Break or waggonette (illus 17).

It has always been the normal practice to put two more spokes in the hind-wheels of a vehicle than in the fore-wheels, but the actual numbers in each design or type vary appreciably from one type to another and also from one region to another. This was especially so with farm waggons in which regional differences were very marked. In the eastern half of England, the majority of waggons had 12 spokes in the fore-wheels and 14 in the hind-wheels, but in the western half of England and in Wales, the numbers of spokes were usually 10 and 12 respectively. Inevitably, there were exceptions that varied from 14 (on each wheel) to 10 (on each wheel) with 12 spokes on each wheel on some types.

There was much less regional variation in coach design. As far as the number of spokes per wheel is concerned, there appears to have been a general uniformity, with 12 in the fore-wheels and 14 in the hind-wheels, and the same number were to be found in the carriages. The great majority of two-wheeled vehicles, whether passenger or commercial, had wheels containing 14 spokes, but there were the exceptions which had 16. So the normal practices should make us look for the exceptions and not be surprised to find them.

# 3 Coachman-and Owner-Driven Carriages

Every activity has had its golden age, when it reaches its zenith. The golden age of coach travel lasted from the end of the eighteenth century until the demise of the long-distance coaches.

Town driving, as a social custom among wealthy people, was not affected by the advent of the railways. Although there were about 4,000 coaches on the roads, they formed only a small proportion of the total traffic that was made up of a diversity of waggons, goods vehicles and privately-owned carriages and carts. There was room and to spare for everyone on the roads and it was only in the cities that the age-old problems of traffic congestion arose. Only through the mists of nostalgia and as a reaction to the present day can the golden age of coach travel be fully appreciated.

It was during the eighteenth century that a great many people of wealth and influence furthered their education by travelling widely on the Continent and so became familiar with the arts, practices and customs of other countries. It is significant that the Age of Reason and Science was also the Age of the Grand Tour. It created an environment of thinking that had a more expansive horizon than that of the parish-bound mentality and it was more receptive to new ideas that were being tried out in the hard school of practice.

The tastes of individual customers gave rise to a great variety in type and design, particularly among the carriages and two-wheeled carts. These vehicles, made for private ownership, aroused much pride of possession, a pride that is still evident today among the owners of veteran cars. The uniformity and stability in the designs of stage- and mail-coaches while suitable for these vehicles would have been ill-suited to private carriages.

Although the Park Drag was essentially a private coach it has been dealt with in Chapter 2 among the large coaches because of its affinity with these vehicles. Although it was often run as a private stage-coach, as an individual enterprise, it is as a Park Drag that we know it now.

The rate of progress in the design of passenger carriages was naturally determined by the condition of the roads, and until the latter part of the eighteenth century the use of private carriages was largely restricted to the towns. It has been emphasised earlier that any attempts to improve the suspension, that is the springing, were virtually wasted until the roads were greatly improved.

As social circumstances changed more people travelled over greater distances and new customs required an increasing variety of carriages. The later trend of the nineteenth century was toward simpler designs and lighter construction.

Most types of carriage had their origins on the Continent, as is shown by their names. After their importation, these types became very much anglicised in design although they retained their original names, such as landau, or a corrupt form of it, such as curricle. There later evolved the essentially English types and names, such as Brougham.

The invention of the elliptic spring did not entirely eliminate the early Cee-spring suspension. The Dress Chariot, introduced in 1860, is of especial interest because the Cee-spring was retained for the hind suspension, while elliptic springs formed the fore suspension; likewise the perch of the earlier carriages was retained. A Cabriolet, a large two-seater of an earlier date, 1820, had both elliptic and Cee-springs combined. The Curricle, which reached Britain as early as 1756, and was further modified in 1820, had these combined springs in the later version. With such improvements in springing and construction, carriages were no longer the over-long, over-tall lumbering vehicles they had been; and lighter carriages, of course, required fewer horses.

During the later part of the eighteenth century and the early part of the nineteenth, driving about town and park became increasingly popular, and it was the done thing to be seen driving. Various types of carriage were owner-driven using horses that were especially chosen for their breeding.

Methods of harnessing have been referred to earlier but to eliminate the chore of referring back they are dealt with again here. Single horses were, of course, driven in shafts. A pair could be harnessed in two ways, either abreast the pole or in tandem, with the wheeler in shafts, and for this the carriages were supplied with both pole and shafts for alternate use. There were two ways of harnessing three horses: either with the third horse leading the wheel pair, or with all the horses in line. The first method was known as 'unicorn' and the second as 'tandem'. Except among exhibitionists, the tandem found little favour because of the difficulty of controlling the leader. For omnibuses, the three horses were harnessed abreast to two poles. It is an acknowledged fact that horses will work much better abreast.

Four horses were always harnessed in two pairs, to which a fifth could be added in trace, when necessary as a 'cock-horse'. A permanent harness of five was with two wheelers aside the pole, with three leaders abreast. This was known as 'pickaxe' and was the method used for the French Diligence, when the left-hand wheeler was ridden postilion. In this country, where driving by postilion was largely confined to ceremonial usage (and to posting) the driving of the various types of the larger carriages was carried out from the seat above the forecarriage.

Driving large carriages and coaches by postilion was much more common on the Continent and we note that notwithstanding the rule of the road, opposite to that in Britain, the postilions always rode the left-hand horses, that were 'off' to continental countries but 'near' in Britain and we are naturally curious regarding this apparent inconsistency. Nor do we know why continental drivers sit on the right-hand when not seated in the centre, although a probable reason was that as the vast majority of people are right-handed the drivers would have the brake lever on their right. This would necessitate their sitting on the right side, where the brake lever was fitted. Bearing in mind that a horse is mounted from the left, we may enquire at what date the right-hand rule was established, or where, because the transition has been a gradual one. New England was originally left-hand, and Sweden and one half of Austria have changed only comparatively recently. It is also not without interest that Italian lorries had until recently a right-hand drive, although their cars are left-hand.

In correct driving, the whip was never used as a whip but as a touch, by which the driver could communicate with his horses, and when not in use the whip was held vertically. It has also been used to give signals of intention to other drivers, by various movements that are visually more effective than the low, knee-level flashing lights that can only be seen by persons directly behind or ahead of the vehicle. Evidence of incorrect use of the whip in the driving of mail- and stage-coaches is insufficient. That some drivers were addicted to the bottle and were wont to make excessive use of whip and tongue, proves very little; only a small percentage of coach accidents could be attributed to this factor. More frequently, an accident was precipitated by an incautious attempt to recover lost time. There is, for example, a monument by the main road between Llandovery and Sennybridge in Wales that carries an inscription recording the untimely end of a coach that left the road and plunged down the ravine. Accidents made news in those days as they do now and the reporting of them was often no less exaggerated than it is today. However, in proportion to the volume of traffic on the roads, accidents were probably less frequent. With craftsmanship at its peak, the standard of maintenance must have been very high, so that vehicles were well cared for and failures of the mechanical parts of the coach were therefore not frequent.

Driving carriages with wheelers alone was comparatively easy in expert hands, but it was the leaders in various formations that called upon the greatest skill and coolness of temperament, in keeping the leaders ahead of the wheelers and maintaining a controlled speed. It needed very little to startle a sensitive horse into breaking loose and at worst into bolting.

Privately-owned closed carriages and large open ones were all driven by coachmen in the service of their owners. Post-carriages, whether owned or hired, were all driven by post-boys. The ancestor of all of these carriages appears to have been the Berlin, either as a coach or a chariot, which had been preceded on the

Continent by a carriage designed by a coachbuilder named Roubo. The Berlin, named after the city, first appeared during the mid-eighteenth century. It was a four-seater, the body of which was slung on long straps on two perches instead of the usual one. The side position of the straight perches necessitated a high clearance to the forecarriage wheels, that set both the coach body and the driver's seat rather high. Behind the body there was a platform for the standing grooms.

The Berlin at the Dodington Carriage Museum shows these features, together with the ratchet adjustment for the tension of the straps. The high wheels are very large in diameter and are secured by large square nuts, a transition between the waggon linchpin and the mail-axle. The Berlin was driven to two or four horses, according to the circumstances of the journey. A fine coach, built by Clarke of Philadelphia, has all the features of a

late Berlin, except for the side perches. They were made of iron and 'sagged' between the wheels to permit a lower body, and had a 'goose-neck' front to permit a good forecarriage lock, but as previously noted the early Berlin had straight perches.

The Dress Chariot (illus 18), in its ceremonial design of the eighteenth century, had the body slung by short straps from elbow-irons that stood nearly vertically from the single-perch undercarriage. It was driven to two or four horses from a box-seat draped with fringed hammer-cloth. A contemporary drawing shows the wheels spoked 8 in fore and 10 in hind, but in later designs the wheels were spoked in the final way, 12 in fore and 14 in hind. Unlike the coach, which had a fixed head, this

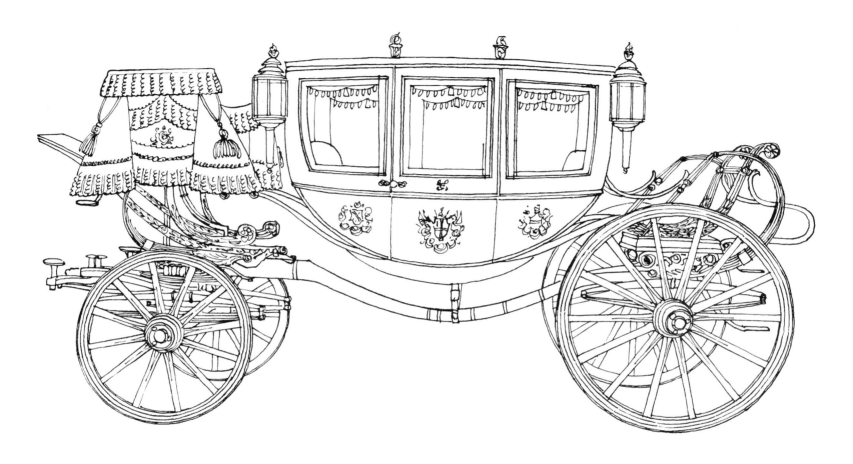

19  State Coach for the Lord Mayor of London, by Laurie & Marner, *c*1898 (Raphael Salaman)

Chariot had a folding head but carried the round dress lamps. There was standing accommodation for two grooms. There was a further distinction between this Chariot and the coach in that the former carried two persons while the latter carried four.

Where the travelling coach had 'blind' quarters each side of the door, the State or Dress Coach (illus 19) had windows in all quarters and was often called a Glass Coach. The eighteenth-century designs had the body slung from elbow-irons on an ornamental perch undercarriage, but the later designs incorporated Cee-springs on a much simpler and stronger perch. The box-seat was draped and attended similarly to those of the earlier carriages.

A much smaller carriage for dress occasions was the Vis-à-vis, that was designed to seat two persons facing instead of side by side. It was therefore a narrow-bodied carriage that presented the outward appearance of a coach and was driven and attended similarly. The Vis-à-vis first appeared in France during the 1760s and did not reach England until about 1820 when it enjoyed a very short span of popularity. The name Vis-à-vis recurred much later when it was applied to an open phaeton-like carriage with single facing seats.

A carriage that came into favour on the Continent and later

found some favour in Britain, was the Britzska (illus 20). With a name that was Polish in origin, this carriage had arrived in Britain from Hungary via Austria, Germany and France by 1818, the spelling of its name undergoing transition in the course of that migration. It was a travelling carriage and was especially used where hotel or inn accommodation was not to be depended upon, because it could readily be converted into a sleeping carriage on long continental journeys. It was much favoured by diplomats and state messengers. Isambard Kingdom Brunel found a Britzska very convenient while he was making his surveys for the construction of the Great Western Railway.

The Britzska was a privately-owned carriage, usually driven

20   Britzska, by Tapp of London (Science Museum, London)

from a box-seat, but on the Continent more often by postilions to a team of two, four, or in certain circumstances six. The compartment extended well forward of the doors, under the driving-seat, to enable the passenger to lie full-length when sleeping. There was an additional seat behind the folding hood. The driving-seat was set very high for a team of four or more and the body was slung on Cee-springs on a mail-perch undercarriage. The iron-shod wheels were spoked 12 in fore and 14 in hind and were built on mail axles.

The Caleche was essentially a continental carriage, carrying two

21 Cee-spring Barouche, by Laurie & Marner, c1898 (Raphael Salaman)

passengers under a folding hood, with seating behind for attendants, and it has been aptly described as resembling a large perambulator. Both the Caleche and the landau-like Barouche (illus 21) were driven by postilions to two or four horses, with a coachman occupying the conventional position above the fore-carriage. The Barouche carried standing grooms behind. In its final form it carried no grooms.

The Landau, in its original form, was introduced in this country late in the eighteenth century from Bavaria, as an open four-seater with folding hoods over both seats. With improvements in springing and construction it remained popular through the nineteenth century, and continues in use as a ceremonial carriage today.

The early design of hood could be folded only partially, but with later improvement could be folded flat. The landau was always coachman-driven, to either two or four horses, except on ceremonial occasions when it was driven by postilions. Originally, the landau was built on a perch undercarriage with iron elbow-

22  Dress Landau, by Laurie & Marner, *c*1898 (Raphael Salaman)

stands and Cee-springs, but later designs had elliptic springs, ran on rubber-tyred wheels and were altogether lighter in construction, indeed some were small and light enough to be driven to a single horse in shafts. They became very popular in this form as Hackney Carriages in seaside towns.

The body of the original landau had a rounded form, as shown in contemporary drawings, and was slung between elbow-irons as used on the undercarriage of the Dress Chariot, etc. It was driven to two or four horses from a plain seat on a perch undercarriage and, like the contemporaneous Dress Chariot, had 10 spokes in its fore-wheels and 12 in the hind ones. All private carriages carried the family device on the door panel. An unusual carriage was a Dress Landau (illus 22), which bore a great resemblance to a travelling coach but had drop-heads that folded. It was more ornamental, and hung on Cee-springs.

The English landau, as originally built for Lord Shelburne, had a square rather than curved body-line, and was called either a

23  Square Landau (Shelburne), by Laurie & Marner, c1898 (Raphael Salaman)

Square Landau (illus 23) or a Shelburne. Later designs, however, had the continuous curve to the body and taking their name from a landau that had been built for Lord Sefton came to be called either Seftons or Canoe Landaus (illus 24). Both types were built without perches and with elliptic springs. The Sefton was not dissimilar from the Barouche in the manner of the seating, but like all landaus it had the double hood. Before the elliptic form of suspension the landaus had Cee-springs and perch, and as built for use on ceremonial occasions had a hind-seat for two grooms.

A later type of landau, c1860, was the Sociable (illus 25), a lighter, smaller carriage, intended for informal use. Like the Shelburne, it had a square body but was driven from the box to a pair of horses abreast the pole.

The State Landau was a ceremonial carriage, driven to four horses, with two postilions and two grooms. It carried square instead of round lamps and like all types of landau had single splashboards above the hind-wheels.

Authorities differ regarding the origin of the carriage that came

to be called a Victoria. It was a carriage that resembled a phaeton as much as a landau, but after its inception, *c*1860, it acquired its name by royal patronage and subsequently became very popular. The lightly-built body had a seat for two persons and was fully open-sided, without doors, and was mostly used for drives in the summer months. There was a large folding hood and most Victorias had aprons fitted for both the passengers and the coachman, to be opened out and buttoned in place when the need arose.

The Victoria in the drawing (illus 26) was built in 1889 and was fitted with lever-brakes and carried lamps. It was lighter than the landau and carried no attendants. The coachman's position was lower than was usual for driving to two horses. The rubber-tyred wheels were built on Collinge axles and were spoked 12 in fore and 14 in hind. The draught-pole had the double-eye head fitted to all carriage-poles. There was just enough space for the family device which was carried on the body-sides, behind the hind-wheels.

All the carriages of the landau group, together with the town

24 Canoe Landau (Sefton), by Laurie & Marner, *c*1898 (Raphael Salaman)

43

25 Sociable, by Laurie & Marner, *c*1898 (Raphael Salaman)

phaetons, were fitted with gracefully curving splashboards. On the landaus this was confined to the hind-wheels, but for the Sociables and Victorias additional boards were fitted above the fore-wheels, forming a nearly continuous line fore and aft with the step. Many of the later larger landaus had rubber-tyred wheels with mail axles.

It was not everyone of means who could afford a full coach-house of carriages and horses. Many people hired their horses on a yearly contract. It was the equivalent of the present-day car hire and was arranged with jobmasters, who kept a large number of horses of various breeds, each suitable to a particular type of work. As with every kind of business, the jobmasters varied in their size and scope, from the very large firms who supplied the big companies, right down to the one-man firm in the village who hired out to local people. The practice of hiring was extremely convenient and many people would hire both carriage and horses for a special occasion. Small firms often relied upon jobmasters for the same reasons as private individuals. Jobmasters obtained their horses from a variety of sources and broke them in to the type of work to which they were suited. Many of the coach-horses were geldings from Holland, where the breeders crossed our Cleveland mares with stallions of Gelderland breed.

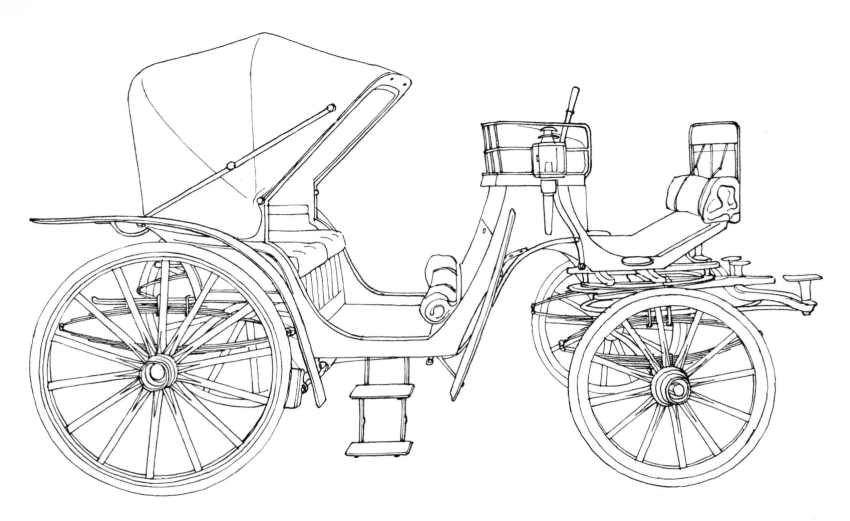

26  Victoria, by Haverton of Newport (Science Museum, London)

It sometimes happened that a horse would very soon show some defect in working, especially with other horses. The first demonstration of 'kicking over the traces' resulted in the horse concerned being removed in disgrace because henceforth it could never be relied upon. Matching sets of horses by temperament was even more important than matching by colour.

Modern advertisements make some play on the two-car family, which in practice means one family-size car and one Mini, but the coach-house of any large house during the golden age of coaching usually housed a number of carriages large and small, together with sufficient horses. Each had a specific use, though in most houses there was the equivalent of the Land-Rover or 'estate' car.

During the latter part of the eighteenth century and after, there was, as has been suggested, some extravagance regarding design and an irrational element in both the carriages and the driving. A young man might 'cut a dash' in the park with a High-perch Phaeton, from which he had to be prepared to jump for it in the event of any untoward occurrence. However exciting it may have been to drive a phaeton to three horses in tandem, the practice was hardly justified in terms of efficiency. But as the more sober nineteenth century advanced, only the most efficient designs of carriage and methods of driving them were able to survive.

27  Post-chaise (Science Museum, London)

The two types of carriage that were used for posting were the Chariot and the Chaise. The Chariot was privately-owned but posted by a hired team and post-boy, while the Chaise was entirely hired, with team and boy.

The Post-chaise (illus 27) was of earlier eighteenth-century origin than the Chariot and was less advanced in design. It was usually driven to four horses by two post-boys. It had no driving-seat but could, in place of the driving-seat, accommodate a large trunk; a second trunk could be carried behind the body, which had

a fixed head. The Chaise was finished conspicuously in yellow and the post-boys (who were men) wore yellow jackets and beaver hats as a recognisable uniform. The Travelling Chariot evolved from the Chaise and with inside seating for two could also carry two persons behind. The example shown (illus 28) was driven from a high box-seat to two or four horses. Like other types, the earlier Chariots were slung on Cee-springs on an undercarriage with perch, but the later Chariots had elliptic springs in addition to the Cee-springs.

The Chariot could be adapted internally to minimise the discomfort of long-distance travelling and could be fully equipped with

46

elementary heating and lighting. Some had an adequately equipped tool-box and carried a drug-shoe for the descent of hills. Otherwise, no form of braking by lever appears normally to have been fitted. The wheels were iron-shod and built on mail axles. Since Chariots were privately owned, they carried the family device on the door panels and were equipped with square lamps.

An eighteenth-century drawing of a contemporary Curricle suggests a marked association with the Spider or High-perch Phaeton. A comparison between the drawings of these carriages shows this quite clearly. Both have the elbow form of suspension that preceded the Cee-spring. The designer of the phaeton appears to have been at some pains to introduce exaggerated curves in every part, including even the perch in which the grain of the wood could not possibly have followed the line of the member. It was indeed perched very high and, being equipped with a folding hood, must have presented a remarkable appearance that greatly emphasised the character of this piece of extravaganza.

The early Curricle was built on two side-pieces that held the draught-pole at the fore-end. This pole was fitted with a T-

47

29  Curricle

shaped piece of iron for attachment to the horses' harness-pads and this was the only instance of such a fitment. The Curricle was also the only two-wheeled carriage that was driven to a pair of horses abreast (illus 29). The later Curricles of the nineteenth century retained this feature and were better designed, with a body slung lower on Cee-springs. They carried a high hood and a tall dashboard and many of them had wheels with rubber tyres, built on Collinge axles and suspended on elliptic springs as well as the Cee type.

Whereas an affinity between the early Curricle and phaeton has been traced, the later Curricles were more closely related to the Cabriolet although this was a larger carriage. It was, however, a distant relationship in both design and time because the Curricle came from Italy and antedated the Cabriolet by about fifty years. But they had bodies of not dissimilar shape with upsweeping curves and hind-accommodation for boy attendants, who were commonly known as 'tigers' because of their uniforms. A major difference lay in the Curricle being driven to two horses abreast while the Cabriolet was driven to a single horse in shafts that were sharply bent. Both carriages ran on fairly large wheels.

A Cabriolet built by Windover in 1830 (illus 30) shows that the designer was at pains to protect the occupants from the elements as far as was practicable with this type of carriage. The dashboard stood quite high and on each side of the hood frame there was a rigid flap that acted as a splashboard when the hood was folded. The suspension shows an interesting combination of

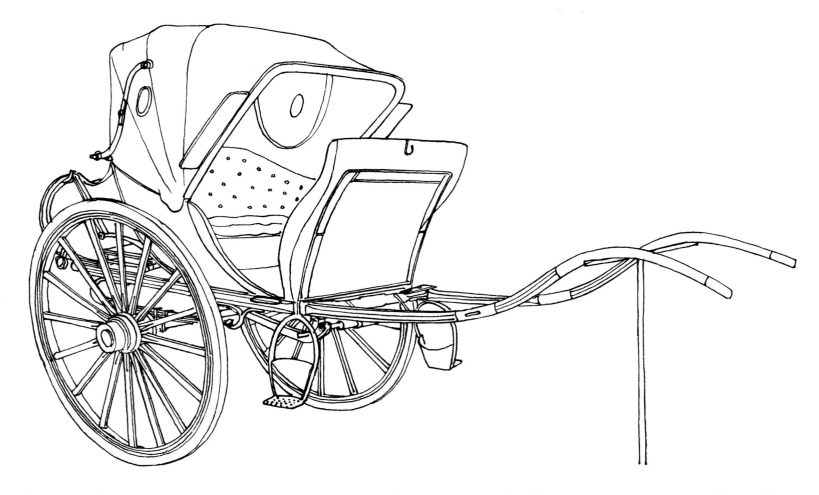

Cee-springs, flat half elliptic and slung forward suspension. The wheels were built on Collinge axles and shod with rubber tyres and had sixteen spokes, two more than was the usual practice for either two-wheeled carriages or the hind-wheels of four-wheelers. The Cabriolet was a heavier carriage than the Curricle and because of that may have lost favour to the lighter and more sprightly Curricle. On the arbitrary matter of affinity it may be felt that the open front of the Cabriolet does suggest a very distant relationship to the Caleche. By the 1830s there was an increasing demand for a less formal and more practical type of carriage for use by persons of importance on various journeys at short notice. It fell to Lord Brougham, who was then the Chancellor, to have a carriage specially made. Like the Chariot, it was a 'half-coach', with two seats facing forward, low enough

30   Cabriolet, by Windover (Science Museum, London)

built for easy access and coachman-driven to a single horse.

The early design ran on iron-shod wheels with elliptic springs, but most of the later Broughams, as they quickly became known, were fitted with rubber tyres, that made them easy-running and quiet in town streets. Some Broughams were supplied on order with two sets of wheels, one set iron-shod for country use and the second rubber-tyred for use in town. Some had a single seat for the coachman while others had a dual seat for the coachman and servant. Generally speaking, rubber tyres were peculiar to town carriages, but inevitably there were exceptions. Many two-wheeled carriages and gigs were so equipped.

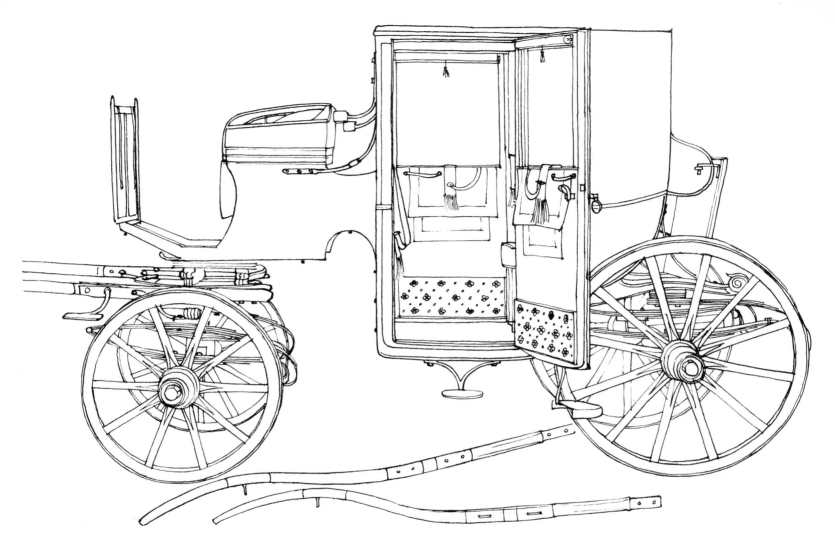

31  Original Brougham, by Robinson & Cooke, 1838 (Science Museum, London)

The original Brougham of 1838 had a closed front (illus 31), but a much later design came during the 1880s, by which time the carriage was much in favour. The new design had glass windows in a bow-shaped front. The example shown (illus 32) was made by Gloucester Railway Carriage and Wagon Company in 1897. Note the comfortable seating for the coachman and the arrangement of the brake lever. This Brougham was designed to be driven to either one or two horses, the pole and shaft blades being part of the equipment.

In 1842 a larger version of this carriage had been built, and soon became known as a Clarence. There was seating for four persons, facing, and there were narrow side windows in front of the doors. The Clarence was driven similarly to the Bow-fronted Brougham. Many a Brougham and Clarence, in their last years, found their devious ways to a long and undistinguished service as Hackney Cabs ('growlers') or Station Flies. The earlier designs of the Clarence had three-quarter elliptic hind-springs and double elliptic fore-springs and were driven to a single horse. No brakes were fitted and although the wheels were iron-shod these carriages were evidently intended for town service. The wheel diameters

were 33 inches (fore) and 42 inches (hind). As with all closed carriages, the door-lights could be lowered or raised by straps and there were leather loops hanging at the door-posts. These features were still present on the first-class coaches of British railways until as recently as 1945–6, when rail travel still retained a little of the comfort and privacy of the Edwardian period.

A scale model of a Clarence of the late nineteenth century, built by Reid, shows the combination of inverted Cee and elliptic springs (illus 33). Unlike the earlier carriages, this design was equipped with lever-brakes, which suggests a change in the conditions of traffic in towns. The wheels ran on Collinge axles

32 Bow-fronted Brougham, by Gloucester Railway Carriage and Wagon, 1897 (Oxford Railway Publishing Co/British Rail)

and were spoked 12 in fore and 14 in hind. Note the patterned frosted glass and pneumatic tyres. Broughams and Clarences were built with fixed heads but there was a variant design called a Landaulette-Brougham that was built with a folding head and self-acting steps. It was designed to be driven normally to two horses abreast a pole. In all other features this carriage was similar to the parent design and had a glass front.

33  Clarence, on pneumatic tyres, by Reid (Science Museum, London)

34 Brougham-waggonette, with removable top (Science Museum, London)

35 Lady's Driving Phaeton, by Laurie & Marner, *c*1898 (Raphael Salaman)

There was another variation on the Brougham theme that appears to have been something of a hybrid in that the coachman's 'front half' was of the waggonette type while the passenger 'half' was a closed body, which had a rear entrance, a closed bow-front and large windows on each side. It was called a Brougham-waggonette (illus 34) and was most likely more suited to use in country districts because it was but one remove from the small bus that was used for station or hotel work. It was driven to a single horse in shafts. We note that on all passenger carriages the shaft-blades were separate and hinged to the fore-end of the futchels. The rubber-tyred wheels were built on Collinge axles and were spoked 12 in fore and 14 in hind. The deeply cyma-curved brake lever acted directly, without intermediate rodding. The barrel-shaped lamps were unusual for this type of carriage which had side windows.

The phaeton was originally a privately-owned and -driven carriage. It was designed to seat two persons including the driver and it ran on four wheels. The original phaeton 'fragmented' into a variety of designs and in consequence the word 'phaeton' became a generic noun for the 'family'. Among the town carriages there was the Basket Phaeton which had a body of woven wicker. It preceded the later and more efficient Governess Cart. The Park and Pony Phaetons were usually driven by ladies within the

confines of a park (illus 35). The Pony Phaeton was the smaller of the two; indeed some were quite little carriages seating one person and as they had no hind-seat, the attendant groom, if required, rode behind on horseback. The type was introduced *c*1830 and had a low-slung floor. Exceptionally, Pony Phaetons were built with a seat for a 'tiger'. Such carriages were intended to be driven to less spirited animals.

The High-flyer or High-perch Phaeton was also known as a Spider Phaeton (illus 36) because of its intricate iron-work. From such a carriage a highly-perched young man-about-town could look down upon the world about him. The T-phaeton had a narrow seat behind for the groom and, finding less favour, soon gave place to the High-flyer. Another member of the family, called a

36  Spider Phaeton, by Laurie & Marner, *c*1898 (Raphael Salaman)

Siamese, had similar seats, set in twin, one behind the other.

After this initial display, the type evolved along more practical lines that led ultimately to the waggonette. The largest of this group was the Mail Phaeton (illus 37), which was so called because it had a perch undercarriage, which suggests that at that date the mail- and stage-coaches were not yet being built with elliptic springs. A lighter version of the Mail was the Demi-mail of 1832, built with elliptic springs, which were fitted to the later Mail Phaetons, of which a larger version was the Beaufort of the late nineteenth century that seated four. It may be noted that although the perch was dispensed with in the carriages it was

55

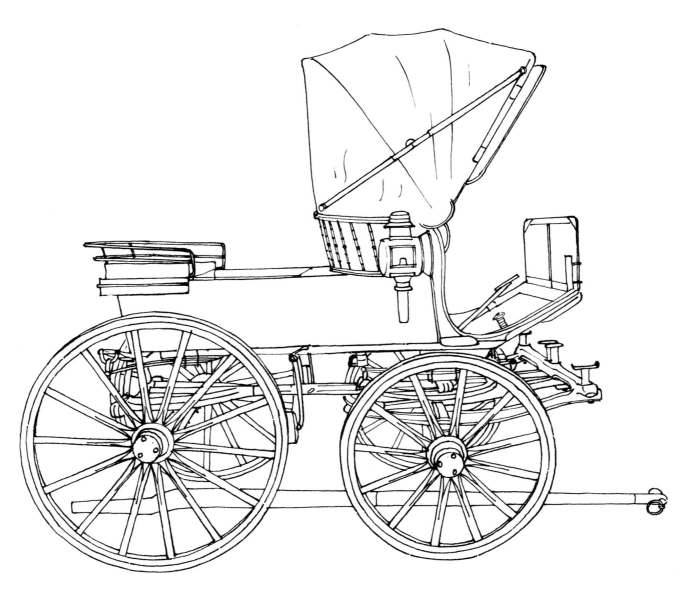

37 Mail Phaeton (Science Museum, London)

38  Pair-horse Stanhope Phaeton (Dodington Carriage Museum)

39   Village Phaeton (Science Museum, London)

retained on large coaches after the introduction of elliptic springs.

At about this time, c1830, another type of phaeton was specially built for the Hon the Rev Fitzroy-Stanhope. It was a smaller carriage with the four wheels closely coupled, giving the Stanhope Phaeton a very light draught. It could be driven to a single horse or a pair abreast (illus 38) and it was fitted with a folding hood and an open seat behind and, like all phaetons, was not equipped with brakes. Some Stanhopes were built without hoods and had spindle-backed driving-seats. The wheels were iron-shod and built

on Collinge axles and, like the majority of carriages, the wheels were spoked 12 in fore and 14 in hind.

A very slightly related member of the family was the Vis-à-vis, that took its name but not its design from the much earlier variant of the closed State Carriage. Its point of similarity lay solely in the narrow body with facing single seats. It was a small carriage and by its structure was clearly late nineteenth century in origin, with elliptic springs and a fairly short wheelbase. The driver occupied a high position with a minimal dashboard. This carriage had no brake and could be owner-driven to either a single horse of about 15 hands, or a pair abreast.

Finally, there was the Village Phaeton, that seated six persons

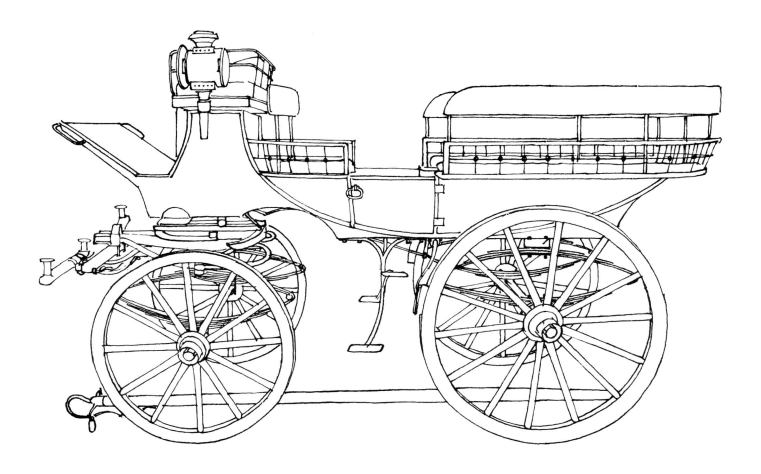

in a manner more like that of the waggonette. The drawing (illus 39) shows an example of the late nineteenth century. It was, of course, larger than a Dog-cart and differed in having a side entrance through low doors to the middle seats. The hind-seat was placed back to back with the middle and had a waggonette-type entrance at the hind-end. The driver's seat was inclined and had no back rest and, exceptionally for a phaeton, it was equipped with a lever-brake. The forecarriage had a turntable, indicating the late vintage, and elliptic springs were fitted all round. The rubber-tyred wheels were spoked 12 in fore and 14 in hind and were built on Collinge axles. This design had to be driven to two horses abreast a pole and because of the middle entrance had a

longer wheelbase than the Dog-cart or large phaetons.

Though the Village Phaeton and the waggonette served much the same purpose they differ in design because of the seating arrangements. Whereas the phaeton had cross-seats, like the Charabanc, the waggonette had the hind-seats lengthwise and facing across. These facing seats were characteristic of waggonettes and Breaks and distinguish them from all other carriages.

The Shooting Break that is illustrated (illus 40) is especially interesting because it has a front, side entrance similar to the

41  Closed Break 'Galloper', by Great Western Railway at Swindon
(Oxford Railway Publishing Co/British Rail)

Village Phaeton, with a cross-seat facing the lengthwise cross-facing seats, and situated immediately behind the highly-positioned box-seat for the driver and passengers. This Break could seat twelve persons, including the driver, and because of the middle entrance no rear entrance was provided. There were double elliptic springs to all wheels. The draught-pole had a mail-coach crab-hook and fitted above the splinter-bar, which carried two whipple-trees for the trace-chains. The iron-shod wheels were built on Collinge axles and were spoked 12 in fore and 14 in hind. The substantial footboard is noted as are the barrel-type lamps

without side windows. This was a large waggonette and not a great deal smaller than the early Charabanc. Like the Village Phaeton, the wheels had rubber tyres and were built on mail axles, but the draught-pole was of the carriage type with double eye. The wheels were spoked 12 in fore and 14 in hind. The driver's seat had a high back and the brake lever was very deeply cyma-curved, and was pushed forward for the 'on' position. This forward movement is noted on p 51. The hind-wheels had single elliptic springs on shackles and a single transverse spring. The square coach lamps had side windows and there were ventilated compartments underneath the lengthwise seats.

It will greatly help us in distinguishing the later Breaks and waggonettes if we remember that, in the last years, a Break was

42 Waggonette, by London and North Western Railway at Wolverton
(Oxford Railway Publishing Co/British Rail)

hired for a particular occasion but a waggonette was privately owned, though usually driven by a coachman, and had its place in the coach-house. Apart from this distinction, any details are more readily to be noted by the informed eye. It does not help us to find that a Shooting Break was an owned carriage and that from this origin the term 'Break' has remained in use.

The waggonette, as such, antedated the Break by about forty years, since it first appeared in 1842, although the Break in its original form was contemporaneous. In this form, it was designed as a low frame with cross-seat for the driver, and used for breaking in young horses. This type acquired the name of Skeleton Break. Then came the Body Break which was the ancestor of the later Breaks and waggonettes. The type of seating with hind-entrance was the most conspicuous feature. All these carriages were driven to a pair of horses abreast. The Lonsdale Waggonette, a privately-owned carriage, was of such a size that while usually driven to a four, it was, on occasion, driven 'pickaxe'.

One more type was the Brougham-waggonette. It had a closed body with seating for six passengers. It was introduced about 1877 and may well have been the prototype for a closed Break that was 'reputed' to have been used by Brunel (who died eighteen years earlier, in 1859). It has much the same austere lines as the contemporary omnibuses and very much resembles a large edition of

61

43   Fourgon (R. C. Dobbs)

an hotel bus, having accommodation for ten persons (illus 41). The style of lettering of the name 'Galloper' is consistent with late Victorian lettering and is unlike the earlier styles. This 'Galloper' had elliptic springs, mail-axled wheels, mail-type draught-pole with whipple-trees for driving to four horses. The inclined driver's seat was positioned on the roof, where there was ample room for luggage to be carried. The springing was elliptic all round and the braking was by lever. The body had four windows on each side. Entrance was at the hind-end. The lamps were the normal coach type with side windows.

A short-wheelbased waggonette (illus 42) was built by the London and North Western Railway at their carriage works at Wolverton, Bucks. It is of the conventional design with hind-entrance to two facing rows of seats for six persons. The driver's seat had the usual incline and the brake lever was pushed 'on' as was normal. This movement of the lever was perpetuated by Leyland Motors on their early commercial motors and buses. The LNWR waggonette has iron-shod wheels built on Collinge axles. They were spoked 14 in fore and 16 in hind, an interesting departure from normal practice.

Many large estates had a Fourgon (illus 43) in the coach-house. It had a number of uses as a luggage carrier and could carry a considerable amount with at least one senior member of the house staff. It was often used at holiday times to carry luggage in advance of the family. The name Fourgon was French in origin and was later used on the French railways for the luggage van at the head of such trains as the Blue Trains and the boat trains. It is the equivalent of the full brake on the British railways. Such a van was called a Break until the spelling was changed early in the present century. So, from breaking horses we eventually came to braking railway carriages.

Horse-drawn traffic outside the Royal Exchange in London around the turn of the century (*John Topham Picture Library*)

A well preserved Drag (*John Topham Picture Library*)

A Drag showing details of harness and the overhang of the seats at the back (*John Topham Picture Library*)

Horse-drawn buses and trams in Manchester's Piccadilly *c*1886 (*John Topham Picture Library*)

A London General Omnibus Company 'knifeboard' omnibus showing clearly the primitive steps to the upper deck (*John Topham Picture Library*)

A Charabanc with rear entrance (*John Topham Picture Library*)

A Thomas Tilling Hansom Cab (*John Topham Picture Library*)

A Brougham waiting for passengers outside a railway station (*The Bass Museum*)

A Brougham outside 'The Shoulder of Mutton' near Burton-on-Trent; note the traditional bunch of grapes by the pub sign (*The Bass Museum*)

W.H. EDWARDS,
LICENSED TO LET
HORSES CABS &
CARRIAGES FOR HIRE

ARDS
DER &c

A Kentish farm waggon and horses outside an oast house having discharged their load of hops (*John Topham Picture Library*)

Bringing in the harvest; these farm waggons could carry enormously bulky loads (*John Topham Picture Library*)

Carriages and their drivers waiting near Torquay, Devon, for the return of a picnic party (*John Topham Picture Library*)

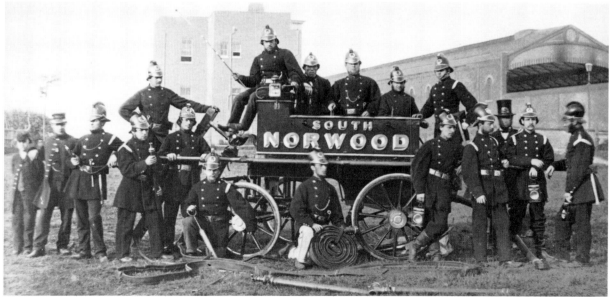

The crew of a horse-drawn firefighting appliance (*John Topham Picture Library*)

A Lancashire & Yorkshire Railway horse dray loaded with bales of cotton, 1921 (*National Railway Museum, York*)

A malt wide-wheeled waggon *c*1914; malt is very heavy and these waggons often had two or three chain horses (*The Bass Museum*)

A Worthington Floater, 1907; these Floaters had a distinctive cranked axle to lower the body and were used for local deliveries of ale, often using a chain horse (*The Bass Museum*)

A Midland Railway Company Float for low loading with a shaft horse and trace or chain horse, 1909 (*National Railway Museum, York*)

A Dray pulled by two Shire horses; this Dray is used for normal coal deliveries (*The Malvern Gazette & Ledbury Reporter*)

A Midland Railway Company Parcels Van (*National Railway Museum, York*)

A Butcher's Cart with well ventilated storage compartment (*John Topham Picture Library*)

A Butcher's Cart on show, showing details of its construction and harness (*John Topham Picture Library*)

A Corn-merchant's Cart at St Neot's c1899 (*John Topham Picture Library*)

An old Devonshire Tip Cart (*John Topham Picture Library*)

# 4 Light Carts and Gigs

Most of the two-wheeled vehicles evolved from the original gig of 1791. This gig was lightly built, with the seat strap-slung on elbow-irons at the hind-end. The suspended 'body' was ornate in line, like its four-wheeled contemporaries. It carried a folding hood, and according to a drawing of that time the wheels were iron-shod and had 12 spokes, but the type of axle is not apparent. The straight shafts were continuous with the side-pieces, which set the driving-seat rather high off the ground. At the butt-end of each shaft-blade there was a step, of ornate design, much favoured during the eighteenth century.

An early development from this gig was the Whisky, that was actually dated 1769 but which became popular early in the nineteenth century. A contemporary drawing, showing elliptic springs, dates this vehicle as post-1804, but otherwise it is similar in design to the first gig. The seat is built directly on the side-pieces, instead of being slung, and although the spokes have increased to 14, the shafts are still straight (illus 44). There is a folding hood and space behind for light luggage. The light structure and 60-inch wheels made a lively carriage; hence the name, 'Whisky'.

A further development was the Tilbury (illus 45), named after its designer, a coachbuilder, in 1820. The body consisted of little more than a spindled and panelled seat with 'armchair' back-rail, to carry two persons. The driving-seat was inclined. The suspension was complicated and heavier, having semi-elliptic springs suspended by straps from a transverse spring support on an ornate

iron structure. The fore-end of the body was suspended on quite long elliptic springs turned up to shackles on the butt-end of the shafts. These were deeply bent and in one piece with the sides, which, in turn, were supported on slender elliptic springs. The Tilbury thus had no less than seven springs. The iron-shod wheels were built on mail axles and had 14 spokes. The steps were of single, plain iron, and square lamps were carried. It is probable that some Tilburys had Collinge axles.

Comparison may be made between the Buggies as they were made and used in England and America, which latter have become more commonly known to us than our own type. The essential difference was that while the American Buggy ran on four wheels, its English counterpart ran on only two. A minor point of difference was that the American Buggy had straight shafts, while on the English version they were deeply bent. Apart from this they appear to have differed little, both having accommodation for two within the body and one behind on an open seat. The folding hood was common to both, although some English Buggies were built without hoods, but where hoods were fitted there was a small window in each side (illus 46).

The English Buggy was much sturdier and better appointed and had much more strongly-built wheels, with mail axles and 14 spokes, mounted on elliptic springs. Both the English and the American Buggies ran on rubber tyres.

The American Buggy, deriving from a source different from

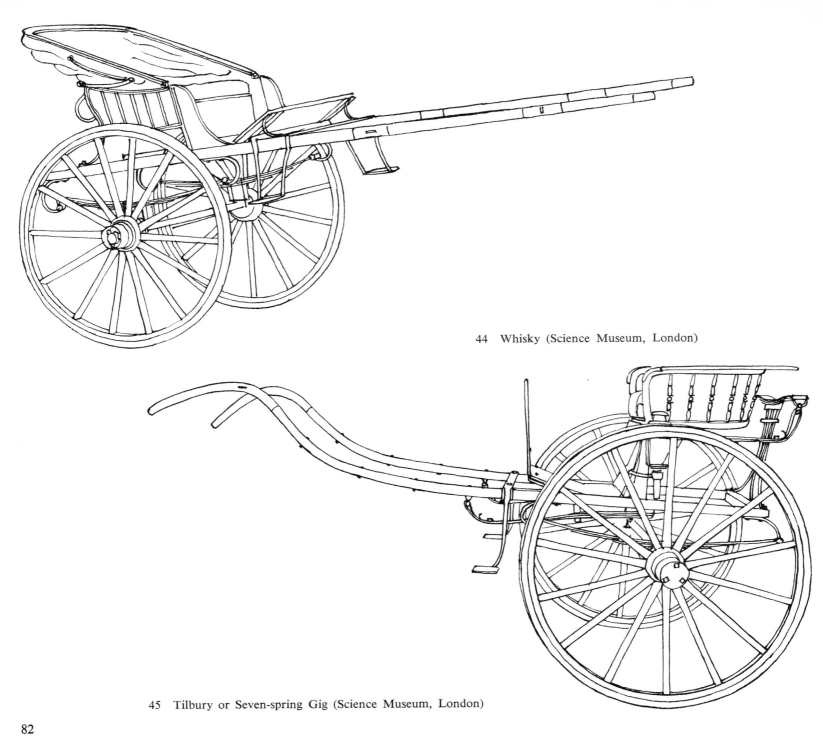

44  Whisky (Science Museum, London)

45  Tilbury or Seven-spring Gig (Science Museum, London)

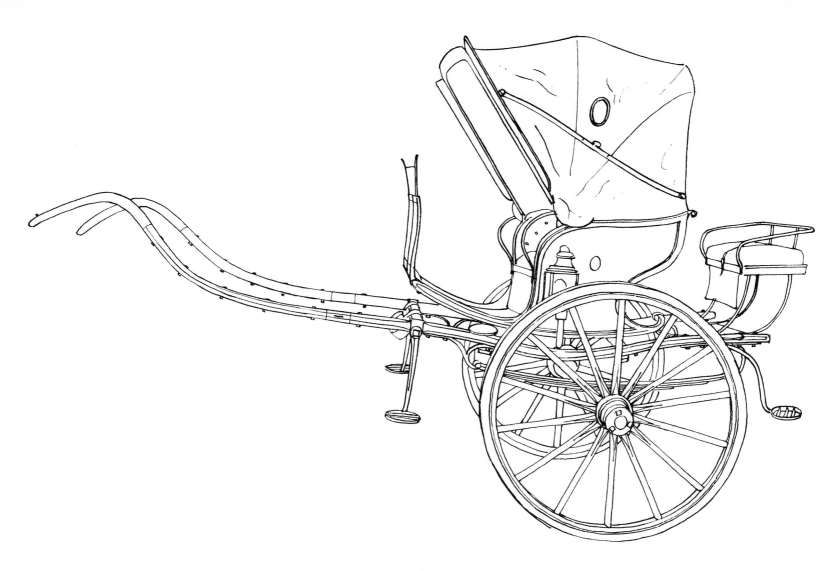

46  Hooded Buggy (Science Museum, London)

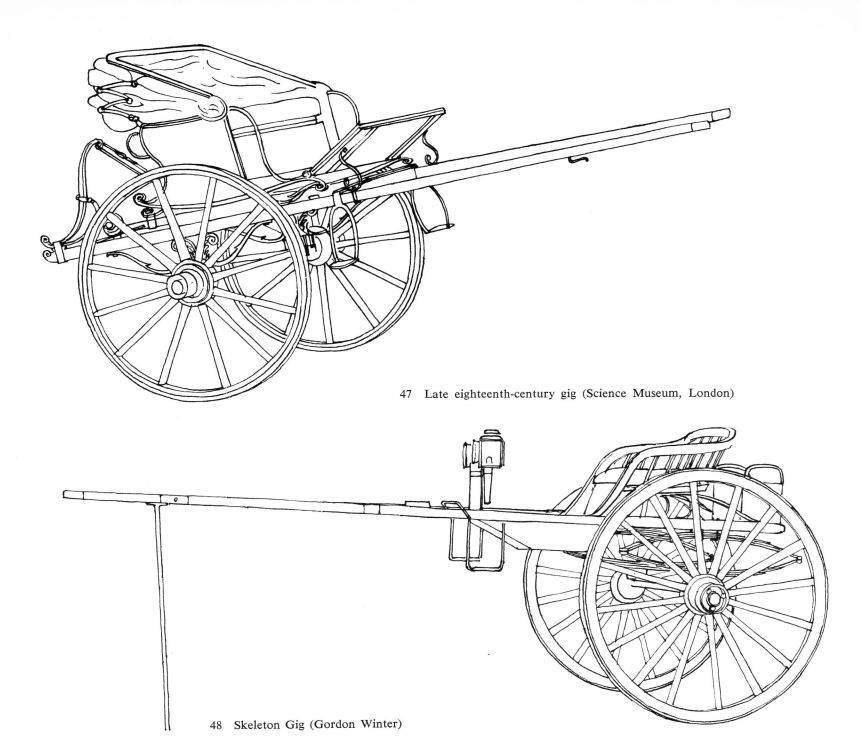

47  Late eighteenth-century gig (Science Museum, London)

48  Skeleton Gig (Gordon Winter)

that of the English (notwithstanding the similarity), appeared in a number of variant designs. They were lightly constructed and ran on lightly-built wheels, which were a conspicuous feature of light carriages and tradesmen's vans and carts in the New England states. A further curious feature of many American vehicles was the similar or nearly similar dimensions of the fore- and hind-wheels—equirotal.

The Skeleton Gig made its appearance during the mid-nineteenth century and was designed to carry a driver alone on a light seat (illus 48). It had straight-through shafts and sides, a Tilbury type of seat without a hood, and space behind for light luggage. The brackets for square lamps were bolted to the dashboard, a more forward position than the normal one on the body. The iron-shod wheels were built on Collinge axles with 16 spokes. The Skeleton was an extremely light and fast gig. All the gigs thus far described may be considered *en famille* in having only a rudimentary body.

A model of a Stanhope Gig in the Science Museum, London (illus 52), clearly shows its derivation from the early gigs, but photographs of Stanhopes of the Edwardian period show a panel-bodied structure with open rails and a straight-backed seat for driver and passenger, in effect a lightweight version of a Market Cart. There was a hind-step and tailboard access to the back with accommodation for luggage. The rubber-tyred wheels had 14 spokes and were built on Collinge axles. The shafts were only slightly bent. By contrast, the early Stanhope, though dated post-1804 by its elliptic springs, has little more than an open seat, and the shafts are fairly bent. An eighteenth-century pattern of step is retained and square lamps are carried. The iron-shod wheels have 14 spokes with Collinge axles. The elliptic side springs are suspended on a hind transverse spring. The Stanhope was

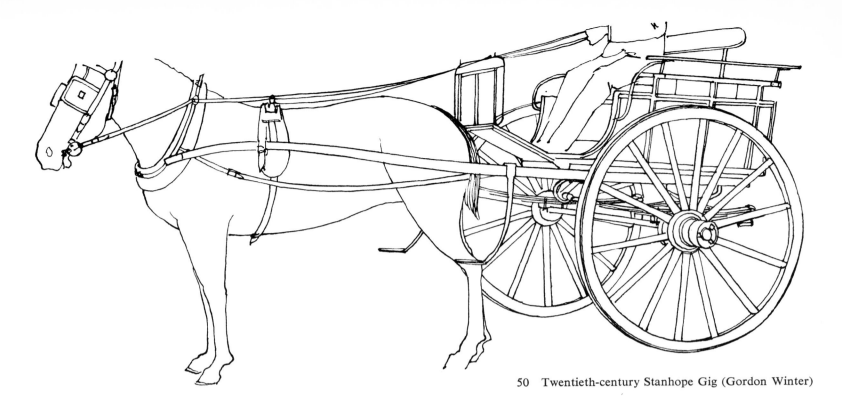

50   Twentieth-century Stanhope Gig (Gordon Winter)

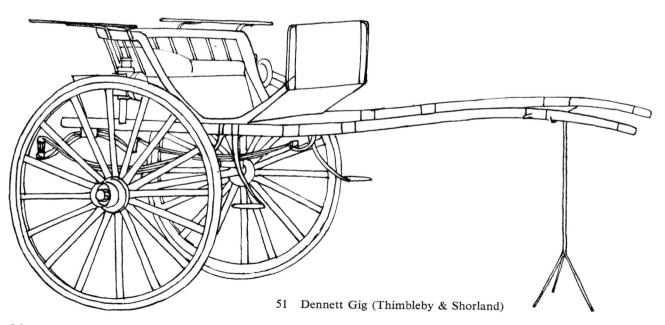

51   Dennett Gig (Thimbleby & Shorland)

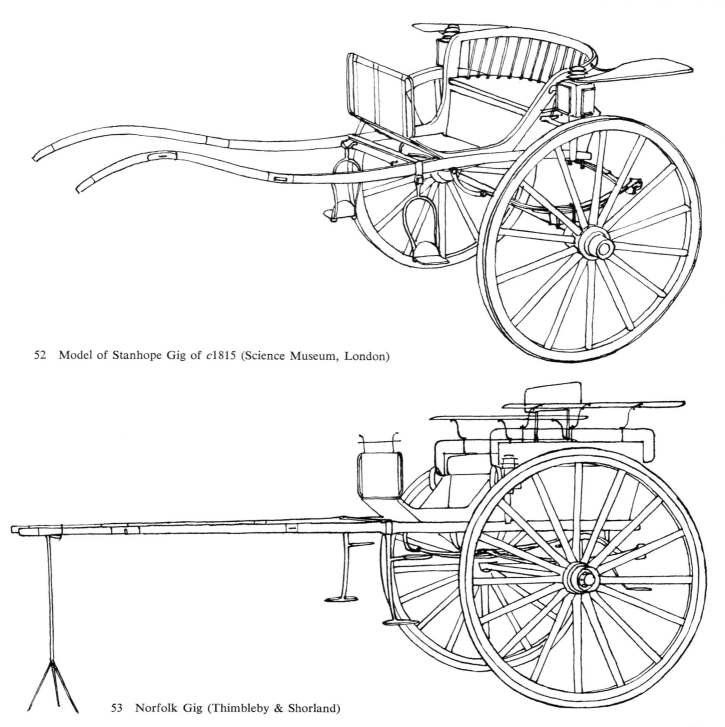

52    Model of Stanhope Gig of *c*1815 (Science Museum, London)

53    Norfolk Gig (Thimbleby & Shorland)

54 Whitechapel Cart, by London and North Western Railway at Wolverton (Oxford Railway Publishing Co/British Rail)

suggested by the same influential person who was responsible for the Stanhope Phaeton.

The eventual variety among the designs of gig was considerable and it seems that its popularity encouraged many builders to contribute their own designs, some bearing the maker's name, some the name of the locality and others named after some well-known person. The names alone are therefore not explanatory, because there could be more than one name for similar designs, and one name for more than one design.

Such gigs as the Liverpool, Norfolk and Dowlais were clearly regional in their original distribution. Some confusion regarding the Dennett (illus 51) is permissible because the builder, whose name was Bennett, named it as a compliment to a well-known actress (or trio of actresses). Some designs became so popular that their eventual distribution became very widespread. The Norfolk, for example, which originated in that county, came to be made in a number of counties (illus 53). It was one of a group of gigs that had back-to-back transverse seats, a group that includes the Dennett and Whitechapel and, of course, the Dog-cart. All of these had low-sided bodies with open rails on top. The largest Norfolk, like the Whitechapel, was often driven tandem. Rubber

tyres were commonly fitted to the gigs in this group which had panelled bodies with tailboards, and carried square lamps.

The Whitechapel came a little nearer to the Market Cart in its use by dealers and travelling merchants. Some Whitechapels, however, appear to have been built primarily as passenger vehicles, with back-to-back seating and an inclined driving-seat. The backward lean of the panel-members was noticeable. The Whitechapel ran on quite large rubber-tyred wheels with either 16 or 14 spokes on Collinge axles. The side elliptic springs had a hind suspension on a transverse spring. The Whitechapel shown in the drawing (illus 54) was made at the carriage works of the London and North Western Railway, at Wolverton, Bucks.

The Dog-cart in its two-wheeled version (illus 55) comes into the above group, but is much more widely known as a sprightly four-wheeler with a short wheelbase and in this form it dates as far back as 1669 as a carriage for conveying sporting-dogs. It subsequently evolved along lines that were suggestive of the later box phaetons, having a square hind-end to the body with back-to-back seating, an inclined driving-seat, and ventilation slats along each side. Some four-wheelers were built without brakes but had the normal lever-brake operating shoes on the hind-wheels.

55 Two-wheeled Dog-cart, by Laurie & Marner, *c*1898 (Raphael Salaman)

56  Dog-cart, by Castle Coach Works, Windsor (A. J. Kirby)

Four-wheeled carriages had shafts with separate blades each hinged to its futchel. Double elliptic springs were normally fitted to both axles. Some Dog-carts had the fore step-irons bolted to the corners of the body, but others had the irons bolted to the ends of the fore-axle. While most of these carts had rubber-tyred wheels, there were some that were shod with iron tyres. Straight splashboards were usual, but some carts had their boards concentric with the wheels. Square lamps were usual. The example shown (illus 56) was built at the Castle Coach Works at Windsor. It is part of the collection at the Kirby Museum, Whitchurch, near Ross-on-Wye, and it is frequently driven. Dog-carts are sometimes driven tandem, but many of them were built to take either shafts or splinter-bar and pole for driving abreast.

The Eridge Cart (c1890) had a very low floor without cranked axles and was clearly designed to meet very unusual requirements

(illus 57). The distinctly 'country' type of body had upholstered back-to-back seats and was mounted on elliptic springs. The iron-shod wheels had Collinge axles and 14 spokes all round, and the cart was shafted for a single pony. The phaeton type of forecarriage seems out of place. The brake lever is unusual in that it is pulled 'on' instead of the normal movement.

The Ralli-car (illus 58) was a late-comer, first appearing about 1898. Because it was small and handy it had great advantages in the busier streets of its day, and it very quickly became popular. It was a country type of gig that was driven to a smaller and quieter horse; a practical carriage it was much favoured by the ladies for shopping and paying social calls. Its conspicuous feature was the manner in which the deep sides curved over outwards, sometimes with the splashboards as continuous parts over the hind-wheels, but most had separate boards with a space between.

58  Ralli-car (Gordon Winter)

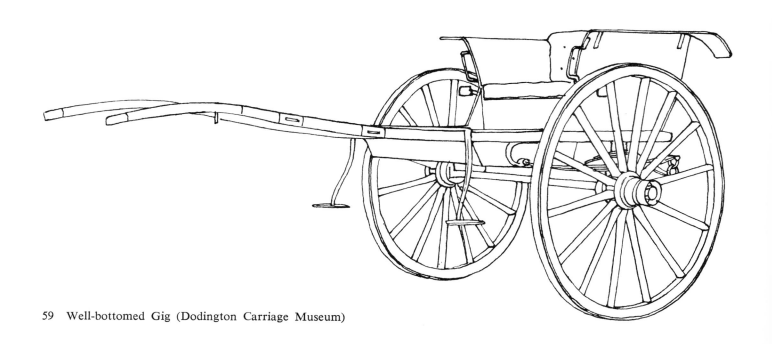

59  Well-bottomed Gig (Dodington Carriage Museum)

60  Governess Cart (Science Museum, London)

The Ralli seated two persons and had a low dashboard and slightly bent shafts. The rubber-tyred wheels had 16 spokes on Collinge axles. A hind-step was fitted for access to the back. The square carriage lamps were a little smaller than was normal for gigs. Some Rallis were built to run on four wheels, with a large body which could accommodate four persons sitting back to back.

The Well-bottomed Gig (illus 59) followed the conventional lines of a gig on a straight axle, but the floor between the dashboard and the seat was below the level of the side-pieces allowing the seat to be set lower. It had the usual dashboard and straight splashboards. A gig of this type but fitted with Cee-springs was auctioned at Reading in 1976.

The Governess Cart (illus 60) was a late-comer, about 1900, but having arrived it rapidly became popular because nothing quite like it had been made before. It was low built on a cranked axle

so that the line of the shafts came almost midway between the floor and the top of the body. It was made in more than one size for driving to a horse of 13 to 15 hands by the family governess when taking the children out. The door at the hind-end ensured safety. The seating was lengthwise facing and the off-side driving-seat was shaped to facilitate driving from a side position, the governess sitting at the back. The shafts were well bent and double elliptic springs were fitted.

The Governess was sometimes called a Tub Cart, presumably because it had round corners and because the occupants sat within as though in a tub. The four-wheeled Governess is unknown to the writer, but one was auctioned at Reading in 1976. Its likely use was not so much for a governess in charge of two or three children as for a teacher in charge of a small party. These carts ran on rubber-tyred wheels with 14 spokes. Collinge axles were

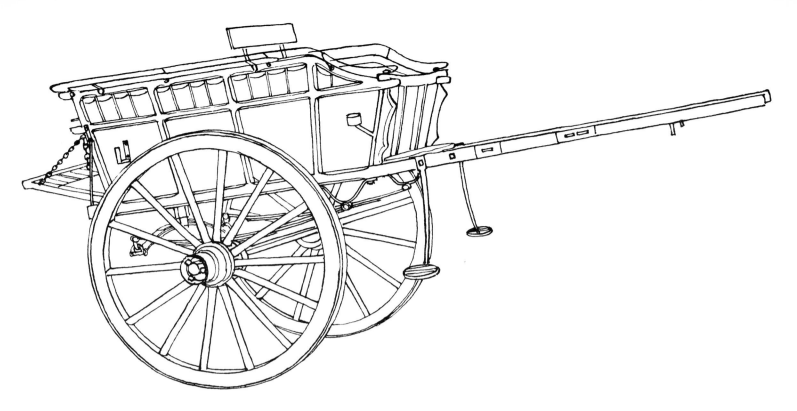

61   Market Cart, by Wates of Cheltenham (J. G. Fowler)

the normal fitment, but some had mail axles. Square lamps were usually supplied, though round ones were not unknown.

Market Carts were chiefly used by farmers proceeding to and from the weekly market, and by travelling tradesmen. They were the largest and heaviest of all the two-wheelers and in their design were more related to the four-wheeled Spring-carts. One variant of the Market Cart was the Manchester, which was hardly different from the Whitechapel and was as common in Manchester as the Whitechapel was in London.

In the structure of the body, Market Carts differed from the lighter types in having panelled sides with upright members chamfered in the wheelwright's manner, and a rail some four to six inches above the top-rave and descending to the rave at the fore-end. The open space between was fitted with about a dozen thin iron spindles (illus 61). Some Market Carts were built with a projecting footboard, while others had no board, the driver sitting within the body. The wheels usually had 14 spokes and

usually but not always ran on mail axles, and were invariably shod with iron tyres. As often as not, Market Carts were made by the wheelwrights in the country towns and villages.

In the Yorkshire Dales they used a cart called a Shandry (illus 62). This was also a Market Cart but more heavily built in the manner of a farm cart. The continuous, straight shafts and sides were square in section and were braced by fore and hind cross-ledges with iron standards supporting the panelled sides and head-board. The tailboard was hinged like that of a farm waggon. A straight rail ran the length of both sides supported by the uprights. The driver and passenger sat within the body on a seat with back and side rails. The open spaces were fitted with turned wooden spindles. The waggon-type wheels were iron-shod, usually with 12 spokes on van-type naves, secured by linchpins on tapered arms. The Shandry was equipped with elliptic springs and driven to a light vanner, with van harness. To suit the load that was being carried, which could be a fat sow or a couple of ewes, seats were often made to slide in order to obtain a nice balance that prevented the cart being either tail- or shaft-heavy.

94

All types of 'oil' axle had a large axle-cap that screwed inside or outside the wheel-box, with a right-hand thread for both near and off axles. The caps had an octagonal nut surface on their peripheries by which they could be tightened by a special spanner. Most spanners fitted one size only, but there were adjustable spanners.

Mail and Collinge axles were similar in having parallel steel shafts with two grooves for retaining the oil. The mail shaft had a diameter of about $1\frac{3}{4}$ inches and was $7\frac{3}{4}$ inches from the shoulder to the tip. The shoulder had a diameter of 3 inches. The Collinge was slightly smaller in all dimensions. The difference between the two types was in the method of securing the wheel. On the mail axle there was a circular steel plate and felt washer behind the shoulder. These were about 5 inches in diameter and rotated with the wheel. Three long square-headed bolts went right through the nave and again through holes in the washer and plate, behind which they were secured by nuts. A mail axle can therefore be detected by the three nut heads on the face of the nave and again by the nuts on the back of the nave. On the Collinge axle the

62  Wensleydale Shandry (Marie Hartley and Joan Ingleby)

wheel was secured first by a large metal washer and then by two lock nuts. The axle can be detected by the smaller face of the nave and absence of nuts, and can further be distinguished from the linchpin axles by the absence of the slot.

Most carts and gigs had either straight or slightly bowed through axles, and on the heaviest sprung carts there was an additional damper spring transversely above the axle. Carts and Floats with low-set bodies had cranked axles that allowed the floor of the cart to sit below the wheel-centre. The term 'Float' was used only for various types of goods cart, such as those for milk delivery and the conveyance of cattle.

The lamps carried by passenger vehicles varied in size and shape. Most of them had square bodies with square fronts, but some of the smaller square lamps had round or oval bell-mouthed fronts. There were also small cylindrical lamps with round fronts. The majority were made of brass but there were some that were made of white metal. They all burned special candles, although we read of sperm-oil being used in eighteenth-century coach lamps.

The shafts of light carts and gigs were very often made of lancewood, in preference to ash. According to the *OED* lancewood dates from 1697 and has always been imported from the West Indies. In Cuba this wood is of the tree *Dugnetia quitareusis,* while in Jamaica it is the *Oxandra virgata,* so that the term 'lancewood' must be a common or trade name for this kind of tough, elastic wood.

It is not known how the terms gig, cart and car came to be diversely used for similar types of vehicle. The Market Cart has, of course, always been a cart, unless it had a special, regional name like Shandry (used alone). The Stanhope, Dennett and Norfolk have always been gigs, never carts, and the Governess has always been a cart or car and never a gig. The Dog-cart, whether it ran on four wheels or two, has always been a cart, while the Liverpool has always been a gig and the Eridge a cart.

In common speech, the term 'trap' has always been used in reference to any light two-wheeled cart (or gig) but according to the *OED* the term dates back no further than 1806. It has always been used alone and never, as gig or cart, with an adjective preceding.

Many light vehicles had an iron loop near the butt-end of each shaft-blade. These loops were intended to hold a long strap from side to side over the horses' hind-quarters. It was called a 'kicking-strap' and was added to restrain an over-spirited horse from kicking and damaging the front of the cart. This strap is shown in illus 48.

In any treatise on horse-drawn vehicles, the terms 'wheelwright' and 'coachbuilder' recur frequently and it is therefore proper to differentiate between the two. The simplest distinction is that the wheelwright made heavy waggons and carts for use on road and farm, and that the coachbuilder made coaches and carriages for all types of passenger transport.

A wheelwright employed carpenters, blacksmiths and painters, but, in addition to these, a coachbuilder employed glaziers, upholsterers and trimmers, and the men in the paint-shop did more exacting work than was required by wheelwrights. On a very large scale, the Gloucester Railway Carriage and Wagon Company made everything on wheels, from railway rolling-stock to road waggons, tradesmen's vans and Floats, farm waggons, military vehicles and various types of passenger carriage and cart.

It was customary for the major coachbuilders and wheelwrights to hold books illustrating the types of vehicle that they usually made. These catalogues were helpful to their customers in choosing the vehicle they required. There were books of large coaches, carriages, small carts, vans and waggons, each book covering a fairly close range. In addition to these books, illustrated lists were made available, while some firms had collections of photographs of every vehicle they had made.

Because the makers tended to follow either their own interpretations of regional types, or to make such vehicles with any variations that their customers required, there were variations in detail that can be puzzling to the scholar. At the peak of carriage driving and vehicle usage, the overall range was very great, and various authorities have admitted to the resultant confusion between one type of vehicle and another. This was especially the case with the coachman- and owner-driven carriages and the light carts and gigs. For example, the London Coal Cart was made by the Gloucester Railway Carriage and Wagon Company and the Bristol Wagon and Carriage Works, as well as by the London makers. Crosskill, of Beverley, made a Whitechapel Cart, a Nottingham Float and a variant of the Governess Cart that they called a Beverley Car.

The commonly-built types of four-wheeler in the group of Dog-carts had right-hand lever-brakes acting on the hind-wheels, pushing forward for the 'on' position. Experience had shown that while rubber blocks acted better on the iron tyres, wooden blocks were kinder to rubber tyres and were more effective. In both types, the blocks could be replaced when worn down. There was a short quadrant, notched along its length, to hold the lever at any position. When pushed hard to the extremity of movement, the hind-wheels were held rigidly since the length of the lever above the fulcrum gave it a very great advantage.

No journey by a mechanically-propelled road vehicle can compare, for quiet thrill and dignity, with a drive in any kind of horse-drawn carriage. And a well trained, well cared-for horse or pony will know its way along every road within a few miles of its stable.

When my mother was a child, living at Eastbourne (that would be about 1890–5), her family would drive out to Heathfield and then on to Punnet's Town, after which it was 'over the heath and common by track to Watkin's Down', with only the light of the stars on an otherwise pitch-dark night (even on a moonlit night, the shadows could play tricks). Neither my mother nor her mother realised that the pony or cob knew every inch of the way.

The family's other excursion was out to Hailsham, and then on to Chiddingly, which they did by Burchett's bus, a horse-drawn affair that was more like a closed break. Burchett carried anyone and practically anything. Whatever could not be stowed on the roof went inside, with the aunts, uncles, children and dogs, trunks,

boxes, poultry (in crates), the lot. Within such confines, no journey was uneventful.

The gig, or trap, call it what you will, was an extremely hardy conveyance for a small party, capable of easy use in those circumstances where the Mini of today is often at considerable disadvantage.

In Sicily, they use a delightful little cart that is hardly more than a pair of shafts sprung on light wheels, with a seat for the driver and passenger. It is lighter and set much nearer to the ground than our Skeleton Gig. A ten-mile lift during World War II, along the north coast, gave me an excellent demonstration of its working and a memorable experience.

An abridged list of Spring-carts, Floats, Luggage and Game Floats, and Market Carts, dated April 1910, that was issued by William Crosskill & Sons, is extremely informative as to types and variations, the sizes in which they were made and the prices. Crosskill's at that time had become the East Yorkshire and Crosskill's Cart and Waggon Company Limited, of Beverley, with a branch at Driffield. We note, in passing, the alternate spelling of waggon and wagon, with a preference for wagon by the

63 Beverley Car, by William Crosskill & Sons, 1910 (Raphael Salaman)

Gloucester Railway Carriage and Wagon Company and Bristol Wagon and Carriage Works.

Crosskill's list shows five types of Market Cart and sixteen types of Float, together with two types of Governess Cart and two Light Carts. The Market Carts, eight of the Floats and the two Governess Carts are here treated under 'Light Carts and Gigs', while three types of cart with straight axles and eight types of Float intended for use by tradesmen, together with the two Light Carts are treated under 'Tradesmen's Vans, Carts and Floats'. The Governess Cart or Car was made in four sizes: to suit a Shetland pony, on 39-inch wheels with $1\frac{1}{4}$-inch tread; a pony size, on 42-inch wheels with $1\frac{1}{4}$-inch tread; a cob size, on 48-inch wheels with $1\frac{1}{2}$-inch tread; and a full size, on 54-inch wheels with $1\frac{3}{4}$-inch tread. The wheels were built on mail axles and it should be noted that every one of the carts and Floats under the two headings were fitted with these axles as standard. The Governess Cart had a high dashboard and splashboards that were curved with the

64 Market and Station Cart, by William Crosskill & Sons, 1910 (Raphael Salaman)

wheels instead of the more usual straight ones. The sides were open above the seats and the space was filled with a row of wooden spindles. The shafts were of lancewood and were slightly bent.

A regional variety of the Governess Cart was the Beverley (illus 63), made by Crosskill. The sizes of body and wheels were similar, but the body differed in shape, having square corners instead of round. Both ran on iron tyres and were similarly priced at from £15 10s (£15.50) to £21 10s (£21.50).

The various types of Market Cart and Float were each designed to suit a particular use and to meet individual requirements. All of them ran on iron-tyred wheels with 14 spokes and were built on mail axles with brass oil caps. The Market Carts' all had straight axles and were mounted on single elliptic springs, with in some cases a hind transverse spring. Brackets were provided for square lamps burning candles. There was an iron step at both fore-corners and three types—the Whitechapel, the Original Spring-cart and the Butcher's Spring-cart—had an extra step by the railboard on the near side. All Market Carts and Floats had fully-panelled bodies of oak framing with a driving-seat midway.

The Market Carts were: the Tradesman's, the Yorkshire, the Whitechapel, the Original, the Market and Station. The eight designs of Float were: the Light, the Nottingham, the Luggage and Game, the Spring, the Farmer's New Pattern, the Farmer's, the New Pattern Spring, and the Light Spring. The Tradesman's Spring-cart had an open front with steps and dashboard and plain panels which turned down to the fore-end in a deep cyma-curve. The bent shafts were of lancewood. There was a panelled tailboard and straight splashboards (called wings in Yorkshire). The large, roomy body had back-to-back seats and was suitable for luggage, etc. The cart was made in three sizes to carry 10, 12 and 15cwt on wheels 54, 56 and 59 inches in diameter with treads of $1\frac{5}{8}$ and $1\frac{3}{4}$ inches. A hind transverse spring and back step were extra fitments. The prices varied from £18 10s (£18.50) to £21 10s (£21.50).

The Yorkshire Spring-cart was made in one size only, to carry 10cwt and was priced at £20 with lamps and cushions as extras. The provision of upholstery and cushions is an indication that it was not a purely utilitarian cart. The Yorkshire had straight shafts and a fully-panelled body with a backward slope to the upright members. It was open-fronted with a foot-step each side and a

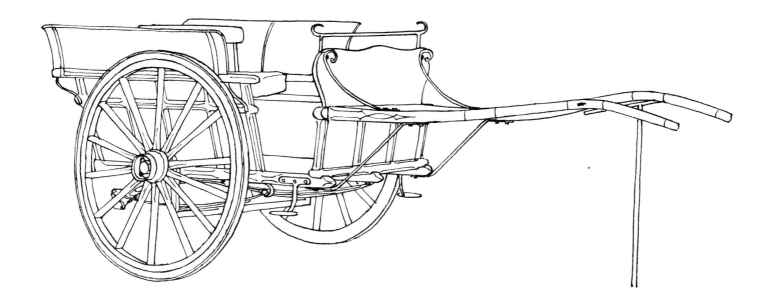

dashboard. A driving-seat was fitted and the body had straight splashboards. The cart was mounted on single elliptic springs with a hind transverse spring as standard. An open iron rail ran the length of each side.

The Beverley Whitechapel Cart was a Crosskill variant of the London Whitechapel and was essentially similar except for the plain sides. Like the original Whitechapel and the Tradesman's Cart it was open-fronted, with the fore-end of the side terminating in a deep cyma-curve to the dashboard. Unlike the London Cart, the Beverley had straight shafts, but an inclined driver's box was fitted to the upholstered seat. It conformed to the London in having a straight splashboard and open top with about ten spindles. The dashboard was set high for driving to tandem. A hind-step was fitted near the tailboard on the near side. The upholstery was of the best rep. The Beverley Whitechapel was made in two sizes, one on 52-inch wheels with $1\frac{5}{8}$-inch tread, priced at £22, and a larger one on 57-inch wheels with $1\frac{3}{4}$-inch tread, at £23 10s (£23.50). On special order it could be built with outcurving sides that overhung the wheels.

The Original Spring Market Cart had a fully-panelled body with vertical members and straight splashboards. The body had a closed

65 Luggage and Game Float, by William Crosskill & Sons, 1910 (Raphael Salaman)

front and was without a dashboard. The framework was of oak with all the lining made of redwood. The rather heavier shafts were set between the side-pieces and were slightly bent and there was an iron step on each side at the fore-end of the body, which was provided with a tailboard. The back-to-back seats were not upholstered. The body was mounted on single elliptic springs with hind transverse elliptics. This cart was suitable for light horses and was adapted for conveying luggage and game, etc. It was made in four sizes, the smallest of which was suited to ponies. A 10cwt size had 54-inch wheels with $1\frac{1}{2}$-inch tread, the 15cwt had 57-inch wheels with $1\frac{3}{4}$-inch tread, while the largest ran on 57-inch wheels with 2-inch tread.

The Market and Station Cart (illus 64) was smaller, and was light and serviceable. It could carry four persons on seats upholstered in best rep. It had a shapely design of closed body with the headboard sloping forward with back-sloping uprights to the sides, and with the tailboard sloping back. The body was built on fore and hind cross-ledges with iron standards at the hind-end

66   Tennis Cart, built in Herefordshire, *c*1900 (A. J. Kirby)

and iron running-pins at the front. The lancewood shafts were slightly bent. The profile of the sides turned down at the front in a deep cyma-curve to the panelled headboard. Optional fitments were: dashboard, back-step, hind transverse spring and mahogany or walnut linings. The cart was mounted on single elliptic springs and was made in four sizes from 10 to 20cwt on wheels from 48 to 57 inches in diameter with treads from 1½ to 2 inches. The prices ranged from £17 5s (£17.25) to £21. The four extras cost £2.

There were eight types of cart built with cranked axles intended for general private use for conveying various kinds of luggage.

The Light Cart or Float was designed for general use and was mounted on double elliptic springs. It could carry two persons and was made in three sizes from 5 to 10cwt with wheels from 42 to 51 inches in diameter. It had a closed body with spindle sides, a high dashboard and straight splashboards. The lancewood shafts were only slightly bent. Like all Floats, it had a step for entrance at the back. The prices ranged from £17 to £20, with lamps and cushions extra. This cart could be used for driving.

The Nottingham Cart was unusual in having a sharply rising front, with rein-rail on the cyma-curve headboard. The splashboards were concentric with the wheels but they turned up at each end. The body was mounted on single elliptic springs with a hind transverse spring. The shafts, made of lancewood, were fairly bent and braced below. The Nottingham was made in three sizes from 5 to 10cwt and ran on wheels 43 to 52 inches in diameter. The smallest was priced at £15 but a superior pattern with nickel fittings, two seats with backs, cushions and lamps, cost £25 in the largest size. This cart was designed for luggage.

The Luggage and Game Float (illus 65) was built with a very low floor, and had an open front entrance with a step on both sides and a low dashboard. A seat for two persons ran along the offside. The bent lancewood shafts were braced by iron rods to the fore-part of the body, which was strongly built on an oak frame. It was fully panelled on all sides. This unusual passenger Float was made in three sizes from 5 to 10cwt and ran on wheels from 42 to 52 inches in diameter with 1½- to 1¾-inch treads. Prices ranged from £20 to £24, with lamps and seat cushions extra at up to £4.

The Strong Cranked-axle Spring-cart was a much larger and more massive cart in three sizes from 10 to 20cwt. The deep body was heavily panelled on all sides, with chamfered vertical member on fore and hind cross-ledges with fore staves and hind standards. The dashboard was of ornamental shape. The axle was deeply cranked to set the body low to the ground. The shafts were fairly bent and braced. The wheels, of fairly deep section, ranged from 48 to 54 inches in diameter with treads 1½ to 2 inches. There was an alternative pattern with iron naves and linchpins. This cart had no seat, normally fitted to other carts.

There were two patterns of Farmer's Float, between which there were but differences in detail. Although both had the same capacities in the three sizes, the New Pattern was slightly smaller than the earlier. The prices ranged in the one from £17 to £20 and in the other from £21 to £24. Wheel diameters were also similar, from 48 to 56 inches with treads 1½ to 2¼ inches. The larger of the two Floats was recommended for station work.

There were two Cranked-axle Spring-carts that were not dissimilar in general design. Both had high dashboards, curved splashboards and cross-seats for two persons. The capacities ranged from 7 to 20cwt and wheel diameters from 42 to 54 inches with treads from 1½ to 2 inches, both carts being made in four sizes.

From the great variety of these carts it is clear that Crosskill's were offering a very wide choice to suit the individual requirements and tastes of their customers. The distinction other than that of name between some of the Cranked-axle Spring-carts and Floats is not readily apparent, until we meet later those Floats designed for dairy delivery; both types were similar in their suspension and only the Governess and Beverley Cars and the Light Float had double elliptic springs.

With regard to the finish, all the foregoing carts were described as being varnished on the natural wood, with the panel stained a darker colour. The wheels were painted, lined and varnished and none was fitted with rubber tyres. All upholstery was done in the best rep, or repp (1860, OED), which was a textile fabric of wool, silk or cotton (in this case wool) having a corded surface.

Similar carts and Floats designed expressly for tradesmen, shopkeepers and various firms are described in Chapter 6.

# 5 Goods Waggons and Drays

It was during the nineteenth century that there evolved the open waggons, carts and drays that were still familiar within living memory during the 1920s and 1930s. The terms dray, cart, van, lurry, rulley and trolley were seemingly used with little sense of definition and as often as not the term 'cart' seemed to mean almost anything on four wheels, and a van could be either open or permanently covered. However termed, they were all robustly constructed to carry heavy loads. The railways used thousands of them all over the country for collecting and delivering from and to stations and yards. From one to four horses were used, according to the gross weight, with the driving-seat pitched high for better control in traffic. The draught harness was of the heavy type with broad back-pad and ridge-chain. The hard-worked horses were well cared for and the railways had hospitals for them near the principal goods stations.

The breweries have always relied upon horses to work their drays and still do, with a tendency to extend the practice simply because, after years of experience with motor vehicles, the horse-drawn dray has proved its advantage. Perhaps the railways will yet return to the horse.

Coal merchants used two types of cart for carrying coal in sacks from the railway depot. One was the flat trolley used for conveying coal to customers and for selling it by the hundredweight sack in the streets. The collection of sacked coal from the depots was made in the London area by the very shapely London Coal Cart, which had a rising bow-front that made it very distinctive. This cart was made in large numbers not only in London but in the provinces too, as in Gloucester and Bristol where it was called a London Coal Cart (illus 67). It ran on heavily-built wheels spoked 12 and 14, on Drabbles axles, with through axles under wooden beds, all mounted on elliptic springs. The forecarriage was designed to take either shafts or draught-pole. The Bristol splinter-bar was above the carriage while the Gloucester splinter-bar was below. The floor of the London was built with side-pieces lapping to form a crooked-bed, with two summers. All wheels were large in diameter, with the fore-wheels standing well above the floor.

Bristol made a straight-bed Goods Waggon (illus 68) rather similar in profile to the London Coal Cart, which had a seat above the bowed front, with foot-rest (which the Coal Cart did not have). The only brake appears to have been the standing drop-chain. The Miller's Waggon (illus 69), made by Gloucester in 1897, had a screw-brake operated from the driving-seat and acting through cranks and rods on the hind-wheels.

The Coal and Goods Waggons were both open-sided with a series of vertical iron rods all round and supported at the main and hind cross-ledges by iron standards similar to those on farm waggons. There was a middle-rave all round, a little over midway from the floor with the space below open on the Coal Carts and partially closed on the Goods Waggon in the manner of a Miller's Waggon. The space above was almost closed by long plates carry-

ing an appropriate inscription in white, such as 'E. Draisey, Acton Coal Depot, G.W.R.', together with a small plate near the main standard carrying the number of the cart, which incidentally (except for the Bristol) had no tailboard. A tailboard was, however, fitted to the Goods Waggon, which may well have derived from some of the Millers (minus the tilt). The Goods Waggon had small fore-wheels turning full under the body. It was principally used by corn-chandlers for carrying corn and seed in sack.

The Miller (illus 69) mentioned above, and made by the Gloucester Railway Carriage and Wagon Company, was the last of the long line of medium-capacity road carriers. It had a spindle-sided body with panelboards above and below the two middle-raves, that were about equidistant between the floor and the top-rave. The out-raves projected flatly to facilitate loading

67 London Coal Cart, by Gloucester Railway Carriage and Wagon (Oxford Railway Publishing Co/British Rail)

when the tilt was removed. The body had a straight-bed and a 'traditional' appearance, although the undercarriage was modern by the standards of the late 1890s (the example shown was completed in March 1897 by the Gloucester Railway Carriage and Wagon Company, for S. Healing & Sons, of Tewkesbury, who are in business today). As mentioned above, it had a screw-brake, with a roller-scotch and drop- or standing-chain in addition. The 4-inch treaded wheels were spoked 12 and 14 respectively, on Drabbles patent oil axles, and the forecarriage was similar in structure to that of the London Coal Cart, except that the splinter-bar carried two sets of shafts. As a consequence of this, there was no provision

103

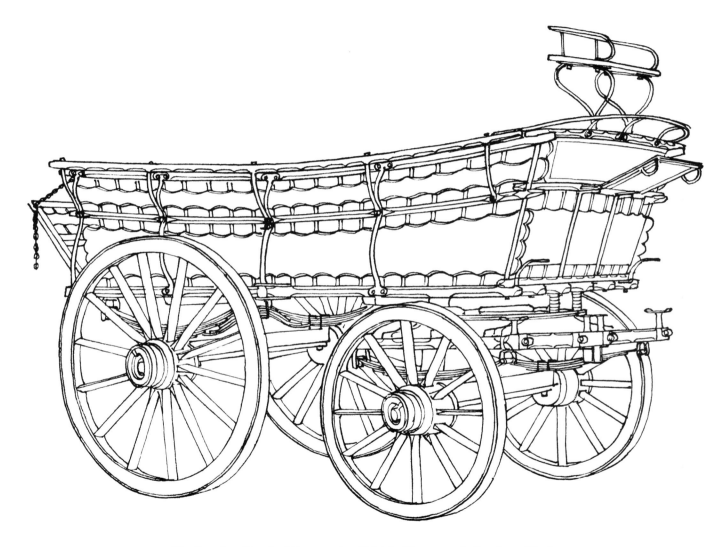

68  London Goods Waggon, by Bristol Wagon and Carriage Works
(John Thompson)

69   Miller's Waggon, by Gloucester Railway Carriage and Wagon, 1897
(Oxford Railway Publishing Co/British Rail)

70  Pair-horse Goods Waggon, by Great Western Railway at Swindon
(Oxford Railway Publishing Co/British Rail)

for a draught-pole. The straight-bed, fully-locking body had four summers. The tilt in the photograph I have is stretched over nine ash bows and it does remind one a little of a small Conestoga though it lacks the pronounced fore and aft rake that was so much a feature of the Pennsylvanian carrier. The body was supported at the main and hind cross-ledges by iron standards. There was a long nameboard bolted between the middle-raves with a small rectangular plate below and a full-width board on the front below the head-rail.

The semi-open-sided carts used by the railways were generally similar in structure and were made in four or more sizes of tare and capacity for haulage by one, two, three or four horses. All had the high-pitched seat and footboard for the driver and here it is noticeable from the photographs that seniority in the drivers' ages was consistent with the number of horses. All the carts had

71 Four-horse Goods Waggon, by Great Western Railway at Swindon (Oxford Railway Publishing Co/British Rail)

lever-brakes, but the four-horse 7-ton cart had a wheel-brake in addition operated on the near side by the 'van-boy'; all of them had the usual drop-chain for wrapping round the near-side wheel when standing. The wheels were massively built to stand up to heavy loads on stone-setts and they varied in tread up to 4 inches, according to the gross weight, and all ran on Drabbles axles, though there may have been some on mail axles. Most of the railways built their own carts and drays, though outside firms very often built for them. All these open carts were equipped with large tarpaulin sheets. With regard to the harness, four photographs of Great Western Railway carts are very interesting. The one-horse cart has heavy-draught harness, the two-horse cart, with pole, has heavy-van harness (illus 70), the three-horse cart has heavy-van harness for all three horses, but the four-horse cart has heavy-draught harness for the pole horses and heavy-van harness

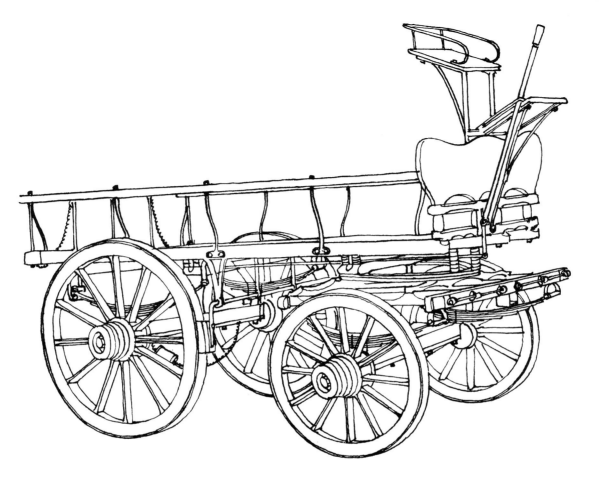

72  South Wales Brewer's Dray, by Bristol Wagon and Carriage Works
(John Thompson)

for the leaders (illus 71). All teams have closed bridles except the pair-horse team which has open bridles.

Brewers' drays have always varied considerably. Some have a series of iron stanchions with chains along the sides, and some have rigid iron rods supporting wooden rails, set high in some patterns, but lower in others. Yet others have a low retaining board on each side to set the casks inclined to the centre and others differ again in resembling a high-sided cart. All of them have the familiar high-perched driving position, with the seats inclined. With all this diversity it is hardly surprising that there are variations in the wheels and undercarriages. The widths of tread vary with either Drabbles or mail axles and through axles with or without the reinforcement of axle-beds.

The majority are intended for pair-horse working and it follows that today as never before these horses are everyone's pride and

joy. When their spells of weekly work are over they can kick up their heels on a country farm. The breweries are not alone in this activity for, among many others, the Solid Fuel Advisory Service has a number of single and pair-horse carts to deliver the goods and their goodwill. Their arrival in any town can be relied upon at least metaphorically to 'stop the town'.

Among many makers Bristol Wagon and Carriage Works made a fine dray with high open sides and elaborate headboard, high-perched driving-seat and a very long lever-brake (illus 72). This was described as a South Wales Brewer's Dray. The Great Western Railway made their own pattern at Swindon, with low projecting open sides and low closed tailboard. It had fully-locking wheels on Drabbles axles with a pole for pair-horse working. The railed, inclined seat was set at the usual height and the pole had head chains to take the gear for leaders when the weight demanded.

73 Corn-chandler's Van, by George Rowe & Son, Edmonton, London (Raphael Salaman)

74  Flat Lorry, by Gloucester Railway Carriage and Wagon, 1904 (Oxford Railway Publishing Co/British Rail)

A great many flat waggons, variously called trolleys, rulleys or lurries, were made by various firms in several sizes. The example shown (illus 74) was made by Gloucester Railway Carriage and Wagon Company in May 1904 and built with a turntable fore-carriage on lighter springs to take a single pair of shafts. All four wheels were of less than the normal diameters, the hind standing well below the floor. All had 12 spokes on Drabbles axles. There was a substantial high headboard on wooden supports, but no driving-seat was provided. Nor was there any kind of brake other than a drug-shoe and drop-chain. It was a very good example of a medium-weight waggon.

Bristol Wagon and Carriage Works made a London Carman's Trolley (illus 75), not dissimilar to the GWR trolley mentioned above, except for the higher headboard and lower pitch of the driving-seat. It was fitted with movable bolsters for carrying girders, etc, and the splinter-bar was designed to carry either single shafts for one horse or a pole for two. The hind-wheels stood above the level of the floor and the fore-wheels below and ran on

Drabbles axles. Both the London Carman's Trolley and the GWR Railed Trolley (illus 76) had the sides projecting at an angle, giving a greater transverse distance between the rails than at the floor. They were heavy vehicles with a peda! brake on the hind-wheels.

Crosskill's made a handsome contribution with some drays and high-sided lurries, the latter being made in six sizes ranging in capacity from 30 to 35cwt up to 6 to 8 tons. All their wheels ran on Drabbles patent axles with treads ranging from $2\frac{1}{4}$ to 6 inches. The prices ranged from £30 to £50. Various extras were available, such as a skid or gantry on which the casks could be slid on or off, double shafts instead of single, screw-brake, etc.

Crosskill's Brewer's Dray had a platform body with stanchions and chains which could be removed when not required. The wheels were built on patent axles and wooden naves at a time when many of their vehicles were built with cast-iron naves (useful for identification because, like all such naves, they had the maker's name cast on them). These drays were made in two sizes, to

75   London Carman's Trolley, by Bristol Wagon and Carriage Works (John Thompson)

76 Railed Cart, by Great Western Railway at Swindon (Oxford Railway Publishing Co/British Rail)

carry 30cwt and 2–2½ tons and cost £34 10s (£34.50) and £37 respectively.

We may note at this point the varied spelling, eg, lurry and lorry, trolley and trolly, etc.

Crosskill made a lurry for carrying mineral water that was quite different from that made by Bristol for the same purpose. The Crosskill had wheels 32 and 36 inches in diameter, with treads 1½ to 2 inches, designed to carry loads ranging from 15 to 25cwt. These three sizes of vehicle had platform bodies with three equidistant open wooden rails but closed tailboard. No driving-seat is shown in the drawing, but as extras a lever foot-brake to

the hind-wheels could be fitted and a pole for pair-horse in place of shafts.

The West End Mineral Water Van (illus 77) made by Bristol Wagon and Carriage Works, was a short-wheelbased open cart, with high sides and a high-perched driving-seat and foot-brake. The body had open panels all round and the fore-wheels were small enough to turn fully under the body, while the hind-wheels had a diameter of 48 inches, with 12 spokes in for and 14 in hind, built on patent axles. There were flat projecting rails to facilitate loading over the sides and the whole framework, of best oak, was very well chamfered on every member. The panelboards allowed ample room for conspicuous lettering.

Miller's Waggons varied in pattern from one region to another as much as did the farm waggons and between the two there were features in common.

77 Mineral Water Van, by Bristol Wagon and Carriage Works (John Thompson)

78  Hertford Miller, by Meadcroft of Welwyn (Museum of English
Rural Life)

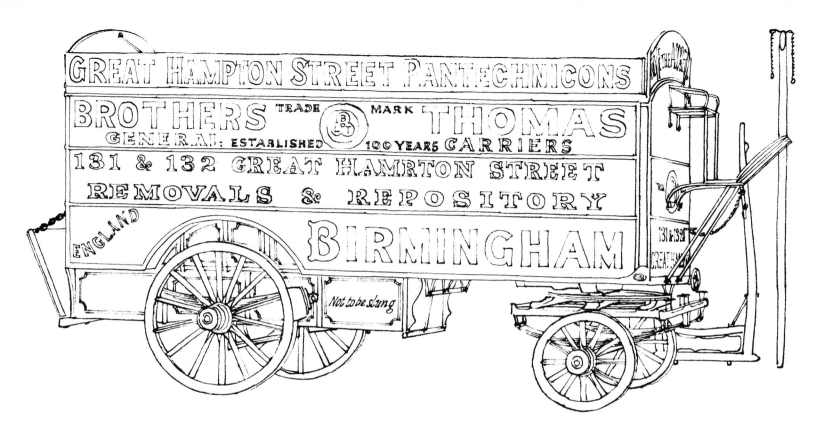

GREAT HAMPTON STREET PANTECHNICONS

BROTHERS THOMAS
TRADE MARK
GENERAL ESTABLISHED 100 YEARS CARRIERS

131 & 132 GREAT HAMRTON STREET

REMOVALS & REPOSITORY

ENGLAND BIRMINGHAM

131 & 132
GREAT

Not to be slung

The Banbury Miller could have been made at Cropredy, since it has the same shape of wooden standards at the main and hind cross-ledges. The round top of the tilt seems to have been a conspicuous feature of nearly all Miller's Waggons.

One may feel that the Hertford Miller (illus 78) was clearly built while the wheelwright was looking over his shoulder at what they were doing at St Neots. It was, in fact, made by Meadcroft of Welwyn and had the same design motif along the sides as the Huntingdon waggon. It had a straight-bed body with closed panelling along the lower part but open panelling along the top, with mid-raves all round. The out-raves project flatly from a slightly bowed front bearing the name 'B. Cole & Son' (of Codicote Mill, near Harpenden). The body was painted yellow, a colour that seems to have been much in favour with millers nearly everywhere, in most counties as far as the West of England. The fore-carriage was made fully locking and carried two sets of shafts. The 3-inch wheels had van-type naves, linchpinned on through axles. The round-topped tilt projected slightly forward at the front.

79 Pantechnicon, by Gloucester Railway Carriage and Wagon, 1899 (Oxford Railway Publishing Co/British Rail)

The Huntingdon Miller differed in having a rising, bowed front end and was fully closed, which was unusual. The body also had a waist-bed and was spindled all round with high-set mid-rave. The narrow wheels were similar to those on farm waggons and large in diameter with 12 spokes in fore and 14 in hind on wooden axles. The waggon was drawn by a single horse in shafts.

A further indication of the variety in design of Miller's waggons is shown by one that has been acquired by the Oxford City and County Museum at Woodstock. This was built by Long, of Aston, near Bampton in Oxfordshire, for H. Druce & Son, of Ducklington. Below the floor level, this waggon was clearly of 'Oxford' derivation, having the characteristic dish and cant in the narrow wheels. The body, however, was purpose-built, having none of the features of a half-bowed waggon. Unlike the 'Oxford Bow' it had mid-raves, set high, with open panelboards along the sides. If this

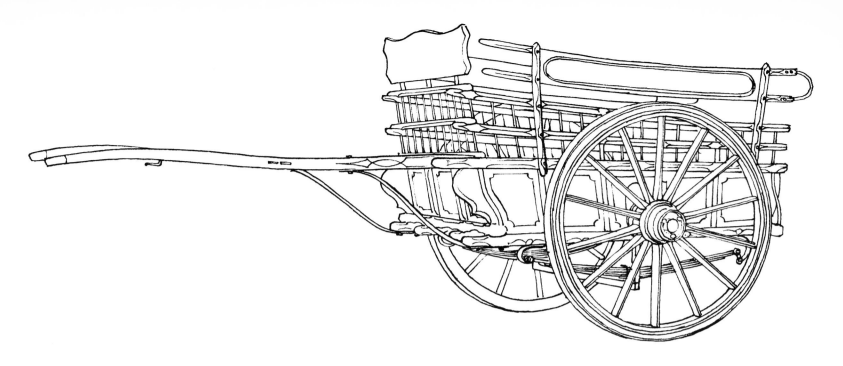

80 Brewer's Float, by William Crosskill & Sons, 1920 (Raphael Salaman)

example was originally equipped with a tilt, it is missing from this waggon with no apparent way of fixing the hoops.

Pantechnicons were a common enough sight in every town and city and their true equivalent was never produced in mechanically-propelled form, presumably because the design left no room for a propeller-shaft and differential axle. There was no mistaking a pantechnicon because there was nothing on the roads that resembled it. The example shown (illus 79) was built by Gloucester Railway Carriage and Wagon Company in November 1899. The very low, well-type floor draws our attention immediately as does the large tailboard that could be let down like a drawbridge, to form an inclined plane for loading and off-loading, and we also notice the tremendous capacity of the body. All the wheels were necessarily of small diameter, the fore ones especially so, in order to obtain a low floor and fully-locking carriage. As supplied by the makers, this vehicle had two sets of shafts and a draught-pole for the alternative harnessing of pair-horses, although the driving-seat was set high enough for driving to four horses when the leaders would be harnessed to swingle-trees. Pantechnicons intended for transshipment overseas were designed to be slung by

cranes, but this particular van bears the inscription, 'Not to be slung'.

One float among this host of four-wheelers may seem out of place, but as it was expressly designed for brewers it has been included under the present head. The example shown (illus 80) was built by Crosskill as 'suitable for brewers, wine merchants and others' and we take this as meaning the retailers rather than the manufacturers. The body has closed panel sides below the line of the shafts and side-pieces, but was open above that line to the upper rails, the intervening space being fitted with spindles. Above the top rails there were two additional rails fitted to wooden staves from the floor level, with a large nameboard above the front end. A gantry was supplied for loading purposes. This pattern of float was made in four sizes to carry loads of 10, 15, 20 and 25cwt, on wheels ranging from 48 to 54 inches in diameter with treads of $1\frac{1}{2}$ to $2\frac{1}{4}$ inches, and were built on mail patent axles that were deeply cranked. The prices ranged from £22 10s (£22.50) to £29 10s (£29.50). This pattern was probably the largest and heaviest of all the Floats.

The horse-drawn fire engine and escape both had very humble and primitive beginnings, evolving uncertainly from the original idea of the 'bucket and chain'. The ultimate in this development was the pair-horse steamer, made by such firms as Merryweather

and Shand, Mason. They were a splendid display in brilliant scarlet and gleaming brass and copper. The engine was the centre-piece at any gathering or event. The early manual pumps were less picturesque and for the effort that was involved, not very effective. They consisted of a pump, mounted on a four-wheeled carriage with the pump actuated by opposite rocking levers, each joined by poles long enough for the team of men whose task it was to work this pump until either the conflagration or they had been extinguished. These contrivances were used by the Fire Insurance Companies, each of whom had their plate affixed on any property insured by them. The business rivalry that existed between these early companies ruled out any pure ethics concerned with life and property; a fire was only attended by the company that had insured the property—and no 'piracy' by any rival was countenanced. Sometimes quite fierce battles ensued between the rival brigades and the heat of tempers sometimes came near to that of the actual fire.

The manual pump shown (illus 81) belonged to the Wormelow Hundred in Herefordshire and would therefore not be owned by an insurance company. Wormelow lies in that part of the county north-west of Ross and the pump dates from 1831. It was equipped with hoses for suction and delivery, brass strainers, a set of leather buckets and the necessary tools. It was even supplied with shafts and a pole for either one or two horses. The driving-seat was fairly low, because of the narrow wheel-track and the lamps were of the square type fitted to carriages. This appliance ran on small wheels and the horses wore van harness. The draught-pole had a crab-hook for the attachment of leaders.

The steam pump shown (illus 82) was typical of the horse-drawn appliances owned by the local authorities of the day and was a common sight during my early school-years. The boiler and pump were mounted over the hind-axle which was deeply cranked on heavy elliptic springs. The gauges will be noted on the off side, but the crowning centrepiece was the large-diameter bell-mouth chimney of brass and copper above the vertical boiler. The large suction hose was coiled round behind the footboard and laid along the off side of the body. Between the boiler and the front there were boxes on both sides for the various pieces of equipment used in fire-fighting and above this there was the driver's seat, with a right-hand brake. While the hind-wheels were quite large the fore ones were much smaller. There were 12 spokes in the fore-wheels and 14 in the hind ones. The medium-tread wheels, a compromise between suitability for road and field, were built on mail axles. A pair of horses could be harnessed to either a draught-pole or

117

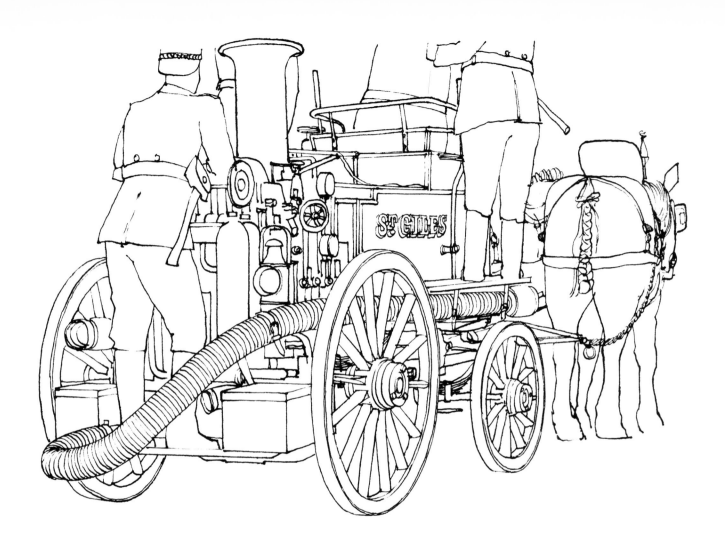

82   Steam fire engine (Edward Hart)

whipple-trees from the forecarriage. When it came to manoeuvring in difficult situations, the horse-drawn appliances had an unfair advantage over the heavy motor units which can be relied upon to dig themselves well and truly in under the worst conditions. The horses used were of heavy-draught breeds that could show a surprising turn of speed over comparatively short distances.

The Dodington Carriage Museum has one of the earliest of preserved manual pumps, built in 1760 for the Dodington Estate by Simpkin of Long Acre. It was drawn by a single horse in shafts but there was no seat for a driver. The insurance companies ran their own appliances until much later than is generally known. At Gloucester, for example, the London and Liverpool and Globe (a merger of two companies) and the Norwich Union had operated since 1859 and 1849 respectively, until the City Brigade took over in 1912. Both of these pumps were harnessed unicorn and the horses used would be described as vanners, with the appropriate harness. The pumps and presumably the escapes (if that be the correct term! ) were both fitted with mail axles.

A note about the lamps that were carried will be useful. The Liverpool pump had square lamps to near and off the driver's seat with a third bell-mounted blind-sided lamp above the footboard. The Norwich Union pump had two medium-sized barrel-lamps to near and off the driver's seat, and two more, rather larger, at the same level above the footboard. All these lamps burned candles.

In forestry work it has been amply demonstrated that mechanisation can only be applied within certain limits, which varied from one type of forest to another and one type of country to another. The woodman of today, whose forefathers used the felling-axe, may prefer a chain-saw, even though its agonised and vulgar shrieks will drown the first warning creak that comes from the tree that is about to fall, but it does seem to be an unscientific way of doing things.

When the tree has fallen, it must be towed away to the clearing. Trained horses have always done this effectively, without damaging young trees and shoots. At this stage, any mechanical tractor on either wheels or tracks, because of the difficulty of manoeuvring, will not only cause damage but often dig itself in.

Light timber could be drawn by chains from the harness, but moving the trunks required the use of timber bobs or nebs, that were sometimes called 'a pair of wheels'. The size of a neb varied with the wheels, usually 72 inches in diameter but sometimes as much as 84 inches, with straked treads of six inches or more. The single axle-bed was massive with a concave arch underneath to take the trunk clear of the ground. A rigid pole extended from the centre of the bed; alternatively it extended from a barrel-shaped drum above the bed. To lift the trunk, chains were attached and wound on to the drum while the pole was pointing skywards. This pole, upwards of 8 feet long, gave an enormous leverage when it was winched down to the shafts, thereby lifting the trunk clear of the ground under the axle-bed. Once the trunk was clear it could be securely chained to the bed.

The shaft-blades measured as much as 18 feet from the axle-centre to their tips, giving ample clearance for the horse ahead of the trunk. The wheels varied surprisingly from the broad, straked ones on tapering iron axles, to the earliest ones on wooden arms. Many had patent axles. David Wray has diagrams of two nebs that were used on the Wiston Estate, near Steyning, Sussex. One has broad wheels with single 6-inch strakes, with the nails in groups of five like a domino, and on wooden axles, while the second (illus 83) has broad wheels with two rings of strakes with the nails in fours in line, on iron axles of Drabbles pattern. The brass caps screw on the outside of the wheel-boxes and not on the inside as was usual.

In this manner, timber was drawn clear of the forest, and then on the firmer ground the trunks were loaded on to the timber waggons according to their size. These waggons (illus 84) consisted of a larger than normal forecarriage of the waggon type with shafts similar to those of a farm waggon, and a hindcarriage of similar dimensions. The two carriages were joined by a stout pole about 8 inches in diameter, with the forecarriage swivelling freely and the hindcarriage braced in the usual way, giving a nominal wheelbase of about 10 feet with an overall length to the pole of about 18 feet. Above both carriages there was a bolster structure to carry the timber clear of the fore-wheels. Both bolsters had iron stanchions at their extremities to contain the timber, which was securely chained. The hindcarriage could be slid along the pole either way, to suit the length of the timber, hence the length of the pole normally extending behind the carriage. These waggons were equipped with brakes on their hind-wheels (which were therefore hooped instead of straked) which were operated from behind by large winged screws.

The timber carriages made and used by the railways were a development from the forestry and estate waggons. As a single example from the patterns of various weight of carriage, the Great Western Railway made a 10-ton carriage, details of which are taken from their drawing-office diagram of 1912. The carriage had an overall wheelbase of approximately 14 feet, with a track of 80 inches over 66-inch flat-soled wheels (a flat surface as opposed to a domed one of two rings of strakes). The diameter of the fore-wheels was 39 inches and of the hind-wheels 48 inches,

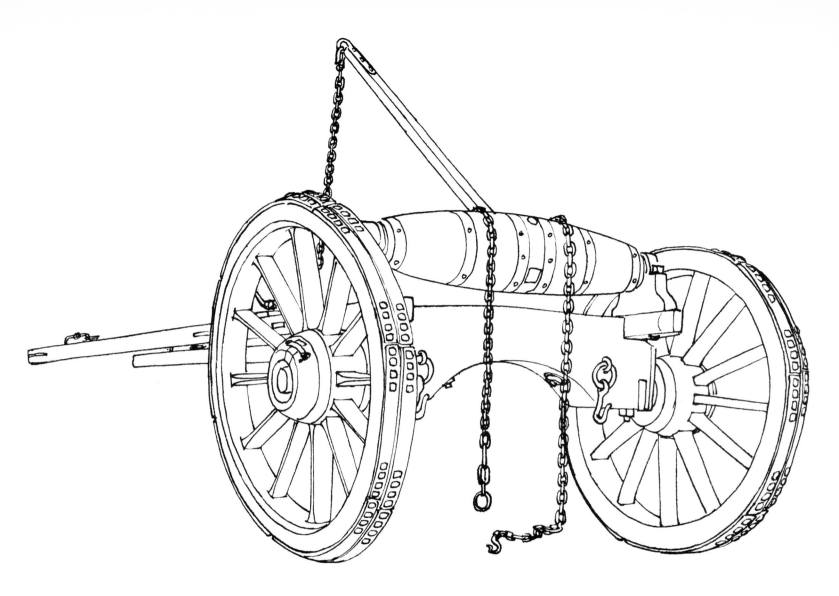

83   Timber Bob (David Wray)

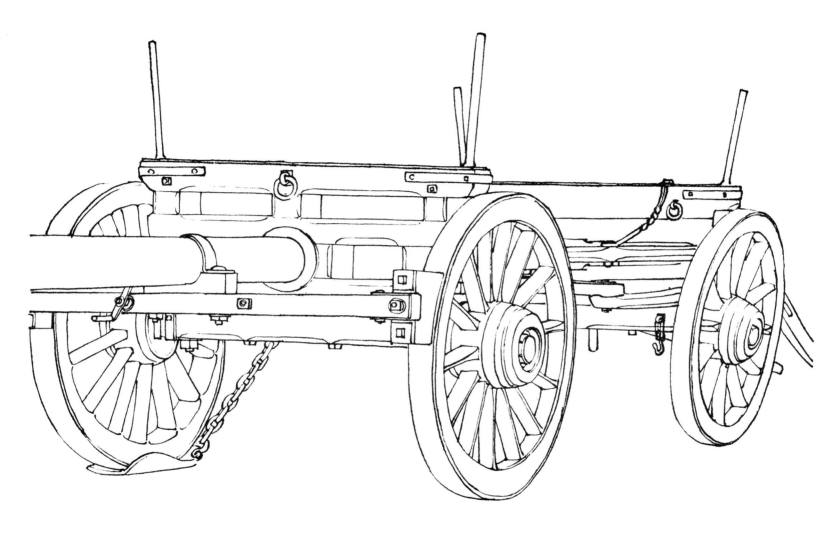

84   Sussex Timber Waggon (David Wray)

with cast-iron naves running on linchpinned tapering axles. The structure of the forecarriage was similar to that of a farm waggon with splinter-bar, but there was a very long crescent-like sway-bar, having a distance over the chord of 68 inches, sufficient to bear under the pole at the widest lock. The fore-part of the forecarriage was boarded over to make a platform for the driver. The double shafts were conventional in pattern. The hindcarriage was strongly braced to take the strain of the screw-brakes on the wheels.

The bolsters above the fore- and hindcarriages were at different heights, the fore-bolster surface being 72 inches from the ground and the hind one 54 inches from the ground, so that the load lay rising toward the front, and giving a better balance by throwing more of the weight forward. The fore-bolster was in two parts, so that the top could be removed to obtain a horizontal load when necessary. All bolsters were strongly braced to the pole which was 24 feet long and 6 inches square and acted as the backbone of the carriage. There were iron stanchions at the extremities of the bolsters, with chains. Additional braking was provided by a drug-bat to the near hind-wheel.

A diagram (number 7117) from Swindon drawing-office, dated 1888, gives all details and measurements of the heavy pair-horse van used by the Great Western Railway. Designed to carry 7 tons, it had a tare weight of 34cwt. The body had an overall length of 22 feet 9¾ inches and a width of 54 inches. The forecarriage was of the standard type with a turntable ring and the wheels ran on through axles with tapering arms. In a photograph the tarpaulin sheeting was spread over an extremely bulky load that would have exceeded the height and width of a hooped tilt, but in the above-mentioned diagram, four hoops are shown. Also from Swindon there was a diagram of a one-horse tilted Float that is worthy of

note. The 54-inch wheels have 2-inch treads on a track of 66 inches over the treads.

The Gateshead drawing-office of the North Eastern Railway produced a diagram, dated c1900, and signed by Wilson Worsdell, who was then Chief Mechanical Engineer. The vehicle was a Coup Cart which in design could have come from any village wheelwright because it had all the features that were peculiar to farm carts. It was actually a shallow-bodied tip-cart, with the shafts hinged to the body about 6 inches in front of the axle-bed. The body was secured by the strap-stick, that was typical of carts made in the eastern half of England, but the side-boards on the top of the body were detachable, with pegs fitting into slots, as was the practice in the western half of the country. In *Farm Waggons and Carts* I have written at some length on the differences between the tip-carts of eastern and western England. The wheels of the Coup Cart were 54 inches by 2½ inches of tread and they ran on Drabbles axles with 14 spokes.

From Derby, a set of drawings of the various types of shaft was issued under the signature of W. A. Stanier, Chief Mechanical Engineer of the LMSR in 1932. It included various carts from parcels to vans right up to 10 tons. In the middle-weight carts of 65cwt to 4 tons, the difference between the English and Scottish shafts is noted in regard to the fittings and the distance between the blades at the collar, which in the English are closer by 3 inches. All the shafts, except that for the Parcels Van, were designed for heavy-draught harness, the Parcels Van shafts being for van harness. The shafts for Suburban and Parcels Vans were much lighter and had no shutters at the butt end. Also the shaft-blades were one inch closer at the collar than those for heavy draught.

# 6 Tradesmen's Vans, Carts and Floats

During the nineteenth century there was an increasing demand that resulted from the spread of the railway system, not only for the heavy goods vehicles but also for the lighter draught vans and other vehicles, for use by the large industrial and commercial firms and the retail tradesmen.

A very common type was the four-wheeled closed van. Such vans were similar in external appearance, but differed in their internal arrangement to suit the requirement of each trade, the individual tradesman and the large-scale carrier.

Almost as numerous were the two-wheeled Floats mounted on cranked axles to provide low floors to facilitate the continuous and quick on and off movement by delivery men. The Dairy Float was probably the most common of this group and comes readily to mind. It proved invaluable in the daily rounds because the horses would continue quietly or remain stationary as need be.

In London, the Costermonger's Cart was a common sight and was useful for a variety of purposes. It was drawn by either a small horse or a donkey, the coster's 'moke'. Such traders as fishmongers and fruiterers used a small shallow-bodied cart on two wheels. The low sides made the kerbside service very easy. The 'barrow-boys' sold their fruit and vegetables from a standing hand-barrow with all the produce displayed in an orderly manner so that the housewife could easily make her purchases.

Intermediately between these small carts and Floats and the four-wheeled vans were the Market Carts, commonly used in the rural districts where there were usually quite long runs between the calls at customers' houses.

There were also the four-wheeled open Market Carts, commonly termed Spring-carts, although strictly speaking any cart that had springs came under this head. With either high-sided or platform-type bodies, they were used principally by market gardeners to take their produce to the vegetable markets. Such carriers were mostly on the road in the early hours in order to be in time for the opening of the market. They, like the Markets Carts, were used where this industry was largely practised.

Many of these carts had an interesting place in the history of the social transition from the pack-man and pedlar to the shopkeeper. The pedlar had gone to the customer but then the customer went to the shopkeeper. The carts so used tended to show marked regional characteristics in their design. The large Wiltshire Cart, to which we will return later, was used by a man who worked a considerable circuit in the region about Tetbury. This two-wheeler was large enough to contain everything under the sun (including the owner, who slept in it overnight)—hardware, rock-salt, foodstuffs, clothing, and so on.

We should avoid placing all the carts mentioned above in close groups, entirely separate from the heavier Goods Waggons, either by design or by use, because there were many vehicles that constituted a transition between the two classes, and even the two-wheeled Market Carts in their lighter patterns were themselves a

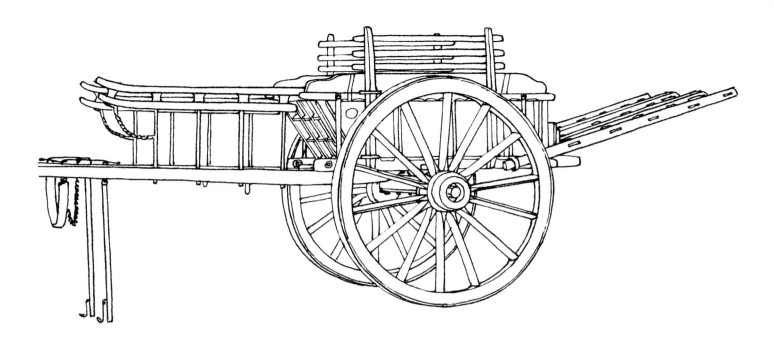

85   London Hay Cart, by Bristol Wagon and Carriage Works (John Thompson)

transition between the tradesman's cart and the purely passenger-carrying gigs.

This means that the way in which commercial vehicles are grouped in this book may not appear entirely consistent, but it will be realised that such vehicles could, in fact, be divided into heavy-draught vehicles and van-draught vehicles according to harness, shaft gear and tare weight. So there were, inevitably, those vehicles that in terms of type and gear, could be placed in either category, such as vans with heavy-draught gear and the heavier vehicles that were nevertheless still geared for van harness. This classification, however, would merely result in confusion.

The railways required thousands of vans for the collection and delivery of parcels and light cases. Some of these were expressly branded for the type of goods they carried and except for differences in detail there was a considerable uniformity in their structure. Many of them were made at the railway workshops from their own diagrams, while many more were made by those firms that were equipped to produce them in large numbers.

Some comparison may be made between the carts and vans that were used in Britain and their counterparts in the New England states of the USA. Most of the American designs appear to have derived from continental sources, because very few of them, type for type, show much resemblance to the British vehicles. It should be remembered that very many of the wheelwrights had come from continental countries, or their forefathers had, and it was natural that they should continue to build as they had always done.

Apart from these essential differences in design and arrangement, by British standards the American carts were much simpler and showed less technical development. This difference was no less marked in the arrangement of the undercarriage, in which the wheels were often of such slender proportions as to make them appear dangerously frail. Even the remarkable Conestoga Waggon, that traversed the Appalachian roads, was very lightly wheeled by comparison with the English broad-wheel carrier. For the lighter carts a tread of no more than 1½ inches was common. We can gain a further insight into the way of life in the New World of the eighteenth and early nineteenth centuries when we note that while the Windsor chair then remained a piece of kitchen furniture in England, this was not so in the New England states, where the Windsor attained a lighter elegance in the living room and bed-

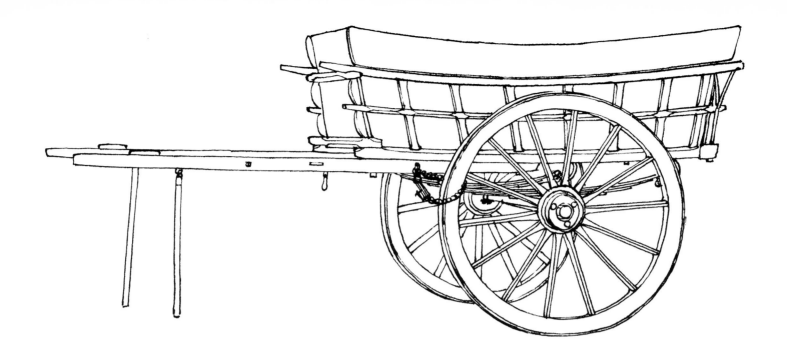

86　South Gloucestershire Pedlar's Cart (Gordon Winter)

rooms. All the men who signed the Declaration of Independence were sitting in Windsor chairs. Fur further information, readers are referred to *Conestoga-Wagon, 1750–1850*, published by George Shumway and written by Howard C. Frey.

Throughout this book, mention has been made of the various types of patent axle, lubricated by oil contained within the bearing by a brass or polished steel cap. This cap was screwed into or onto the wheel-box, thereby revolving with the wheel. Because of this free rotation, all caps had right-hand threads whether for the near or off axle.

Of the three types, the mail, the Drabbles and the Collinge, it was the first that was commonly fitted on vans, carts and Floats, although a small number had Collinge axles. The latter was fitted to naves of smaller diameter so that it was easy to distinguish at a glance these wheels from the mail-axled wheels, which had larger diameter naves to accommodate the three bolts. The rings on the noses of the naves, made of brass, corresponded to the size of the naves. It may be noted that on such farm waggons, etc, that had these rings the term 'van-nave' was used to distinguish this type from the older type that had a full slot with wooden stopper. The van-nave also had a slot, within the ring, just large enough to permit insertion and extraction of the small linchpin.

The Drabbles type of axle was tapered, the mail and Collinge being parallel, and usually had a cap of polished steel. As has earlier been stated, the oil cap had an octagonal nut on its surface to allow adjustment by a suitable spanner, though occasionally one came across a light vehicle with hexagonal nuts.

Brass caps were, of course, more easily kept polished than were steel ones and this all helped to make the van look smart. The metal rings were likewise made of brass, and they usually had a bell-shaped mouth.

In work on the farm there had been some objection in the past to the oil cap. It arose because some waggoners of the 'old school' either managed to cross the threads or lose the caps because they had not tightened them sufficiently. This may be an apocryphal story, but among owners and users of carriages with mail or Collinge axles, no objection was ever known to be raised; perhaps they were more sophisticated and were proud of their vehicles.

The wheels on the later road vehicles of all kinds, whether for heavy or lighter draught, were all built with the spokes 'staggered', that is, set alternately in and out around the nave, to give added strength to wheels built with a very shallow dish. These vehicles

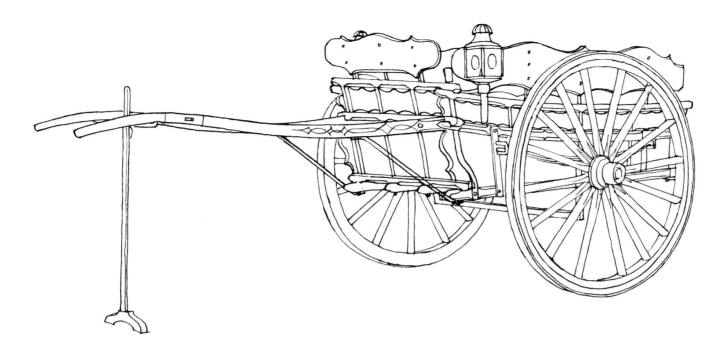

87 Midland Float, by William Crosskill & Sons, 1910 (Raphael Salaman)

ran more lightly on a good road and were far less subject to the lateral stresses that constantly occurred with farm vehicles.

There have been many academic arguments on the matter of cant and dish that might never have arisen had wheels always run on perfect surfaces, but even a steep camber can throw the weight to one side. The undulations that develop on a wearing road surface will set up various stresses that can be counteracted by a slight dish.

The shafts that were usually fitted to tradesmen's vans and Floats were of lighter construction than those for the heavy-draught vehicles which had shafts like those on farm waggons. These van shafts were sometimes of the 'bent' type rather than the straight, though never to the same extent as the exaggerated curves found in the shafts of carriages and gigs. The original idea of the bent shaft was to bring the point of attachment to the loop in the harness, where the carriage was generally of a lower build. Nevertheless, it will be noticed that some bent shafts were more sharply curved than others. The shafts for heavy-draught gear had the long staple and swivelling hooks to which the ridge-chain was attached, but on van shafts this staple was replaced by a metal peg that projected laterally to secure the loop on the harness that passed around the shaft-blade.

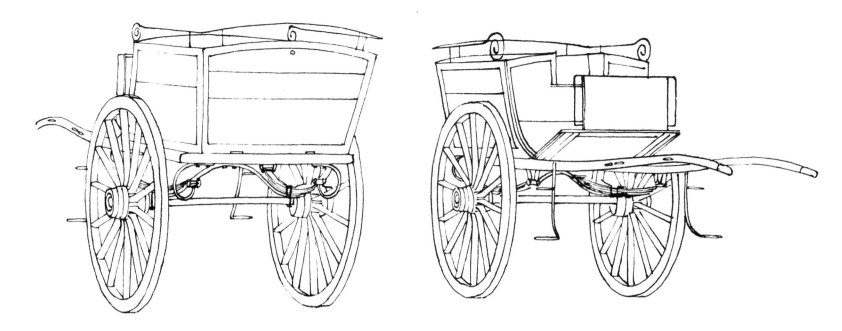

The list of diagrams and photographs so far available from the joint venture of Oxford Railway Publishing Company and British Rail is already considerable. Eventually this list will extend to include most of the types of vehicle used by the railways whether made by the railway companies themselves or by contracting carriage and waggon builders. Together, they will form a vast source for active modellers and passive students. We are indebted to the railways for keeping these records. The great value of the diagrams lies partly in such details as the number of leaves in the springs, the dates, and also that they are to the modelling scale of 1:8.

The Gloucester Railway Carriage and Wagon Company made a considerable range of vehicles for tradesmen, firms and the railway. A Parcels Van for the Great Central Railway had a rectangular body with a slight canopy (illus 89). The footboard had a dashboard, but no kind of brake is apparent in the photograph. On each side of the seat there was an oval window, set high in the body. The roof had rails all round, with straps to contain additional parcels. At the hind-end there was a double door. The makers had a standard pattern of forecarriage, with twin pillows and turntable ring with futchels of iron to take the splinter-bar, reminiscent of the style of the phaetons. The splinter-bar was

88   Ice-cream carts, by Gloucester Railway Carriage and Wagon, 1897 (Oxford Railway Publishing Co/British Rail)

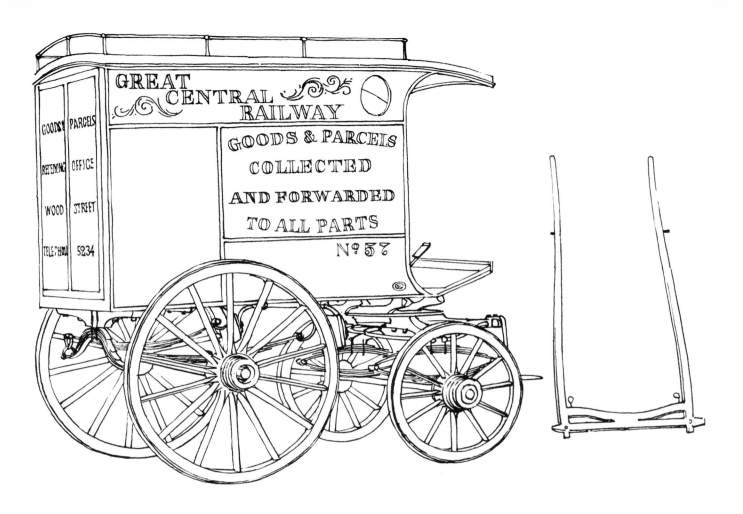

89 Railway Parcels Van, by Gloucester Railway Carriage and Wagon, 1898 (Oxford Railway Publishing Co/British Rail)

designed to carry both shafts and pole for one or two horses according to the load or the road. The shaft-blades tapered off to a light section at the toes. An iron step was attached to the extremities of the splinter-bar. The forecarriage was mounted on double elliptic springs but the hind-end was mounted on the usual single springs, suspended by a transverse spring at the rear. It was the usual practice to have the fore-wheels small enough for a full lock with the hind-wheels tall enough to stand well above the floor. They were spoked 12 in fore and 14 in hind and built on mail axles with the letters GCR incised on the oil caps. This van was part of an order carried out in 1898.

A Delivery Van for Coventry Perseverance Co-operative Society was one of a number built in 1896. It had similar carriage

structure to the GCR Van, but its shafts were gently bent. The
fore-steps were bolted to the fore-axles and had to be removed in
order to remove the oil caps. Quite a number of vans and carts
were made with this type of step instead of the pattern that was
bolted to the splinter-bar. The Coventry body had a more
extended canopy with an elaborately cut frontboard and the footboard carried a dashboard. Square carriage lamps were carried.
The commonly fitted transverse hind-spring was not fitted to this
van.

Gloucester made a nice Baker's Van for Edward Moss, of
Spark Hill, that strongly echoed a phaeton in the shape of its body
(illus 90). This was cut away behind the pillows to allow ample
room for the much larger wheels at full lock. Otherwise, this van

90   Baker's Cart, by Gloucester Railway Carriage and Wagon (Oxford
Railway Publishing Co/British Rail)

129

91  Brewer's Covered Van, by Gloucester Railway Carriage and
    Wagon (Oxford Railway Publishing Co/British Rail)

was similar to the others in respect of the undercarriage, but was fitted with a pedal-brake. The designer of the body was apparently at some pains to produce a van that could well have graced the coach-house of some big mansion. It was equipped with carriage lamps and one may observe that the lettering was of the standard that one came to associate with the company which made it.

They made a heavier type of van in 1897 for the Stroud Brewery Company, for pair-horse working in shafts, which was attached to a more robust waggon-type forecarriage (illus 91). This had elliptic springs. The wheels too were of a heavier build with Drabbles axles. The shafts were of the heavy-draught type with hooks for trace chains when extra horses were required for the hills that lie about the Stroud valley. A screw-brake and roller-scotch indicate the nature of those hills. The body was strongly built with iron standards and cross-ledges, and was equipped with a canvas tilt on seven hoops with a forward projection.

Pure ice was delivered by the Malvern Water Company of Colwall in light two-wheeled carts, made in 1897. They were an adaptation of the Market Cart with an open front and dashboard and hind-doors. The large wheels were built on mail axles with 14 spokes. The shafts were fairly bent to a light-van harness. The single elliptic springs were hung from scroll-irons at the hind-end.

Gloucester also made a shapely Float in 1893 for diverse use that in its general shape seems to have stemmed from some of the lighter farm carts. The shafts were slightly bent and lap-joined to the main side-pieces, below which the panelboards closed the body, while above there was a row of 17 spindles, backed by open panelling. The front was constructed similarly and had a high elaborate headboard braced by irons with involute spirals. The

92  Butcher's Cart, by William Crosskill & Sons, 1910 (Raphael
Salaman)

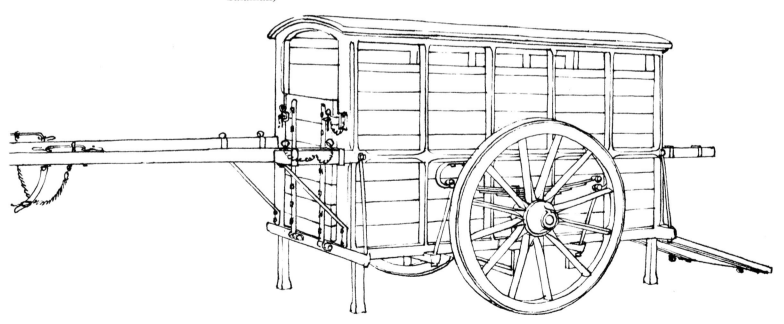

93  Cranked-axle Cattle Cart (or Bull Float), by Bristol Wagon and
Carriage Works (John Thompson)

131

94 Builder's Cart, by Gloucester Railway Carriage and Wagon, 1896 (Oxford Railway Publishing Co/British Rail)

large wheels had 14 spokes on mail axles, hung on a deeply cranked axle.

Various patterns of open light or medium cart were made at this period. Tipping carts for the Great Western Railway were similar, with the shafts hinged to the body well forward of the axle line. The bent shafts were made for medium-heavy draught and the wheels had Drabbles axles and large wooden naves. Both designs had springs.

A lighter cart for van draught was made for William James, a Malvern builder (illus 94). The panelled body was nicely chamfered with a large headboard braced by ornate iron-work. The body was mounted on springs to a through–axle bolted to an axle-bed (absent from the GWR carts). The wheels had 14 spokes on mail axles and the van-shafts were straight.

The list issued by the Bristol Wagon and Carriage Works Company in 1901 showed a diverse range. The closed vans were similar to the Gloucester patterns but were clearly shown to be fitted with lever-brakes, and all ran on mail axles. Their open vans were made in two sizes, for cob and pony, to carry up to 1 and 1½ tons, and were priced up to £38. The backward rake of the body made them look very attractive. They were designed for collection and delivery at railway stations.

The Bristol list showed nine patterns of Milk Float on cranked axles, the most interesting being a 'New Pattern' with Warner wheels and Collinge axles, for pony size, to carry either 12-gallon or 16-gallon churns with brass mountings and taps, as extras, at an inclusive price up to £27 5s (£27.25). They also had a Light Spring-float, for dairy work, that had rising railed sides, surmounted by an ornamental headboard carrying carriage lamps.

A Cranked-axle Cattle Cart, used by stockbreeders, was built for entry and exit at each end, with removable shafts (illus 93). It had a wooden covered top.

The Crosskill list for 1910 showed a similar diversity among which was a Brewer's Float intended for merchants' use. It was both ornate and practical, with open rails above the side-pieces and a closed body below. It was made in four sizes from 10 to 25cwt, on wheels of 48 and 54 inches diameter with treads from 1½ to 2¼ inches. It ran on mail axles. A Midland Float was more lightly built on Collinge axles to carry 10 or 15cwt.

Bristol made three patterns of Milk Float, called a Jersey, an Alderney and a Manchester. The Jersey (illus 95) was conventional in design, with a low hind-step that could be raised to form a tailboard, but the Alderney was unusual in having a low front entry with a dashboard.

Two very handy light carts were made by Crosskill in their 1910 list. One was designed for fishmongers with low sides (illus 96), and the other for fruiterers, with higher railed sides (illus 97).

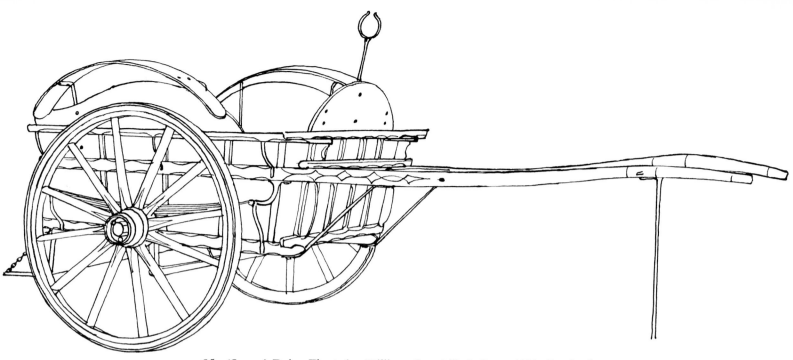

95 'Jersey' Dairy Float, by William Crosskill & Sons, 1910 (Raphael Salaman)

96 Fishmonger's Cart, by William Crosskill & Sons, 1910 (Raphael Salaman)

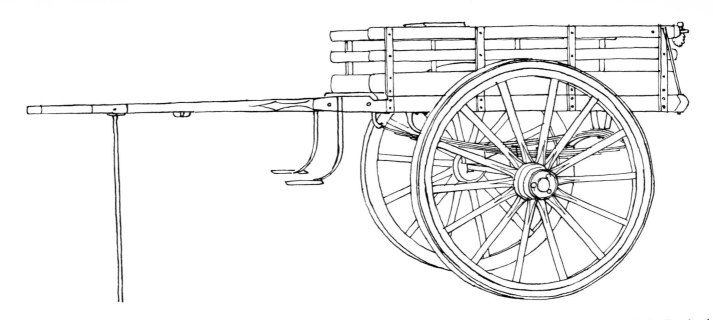

97 Fruiterer's Cart, by William Crosskill & Sons, 1910 (Raphael Salaman)

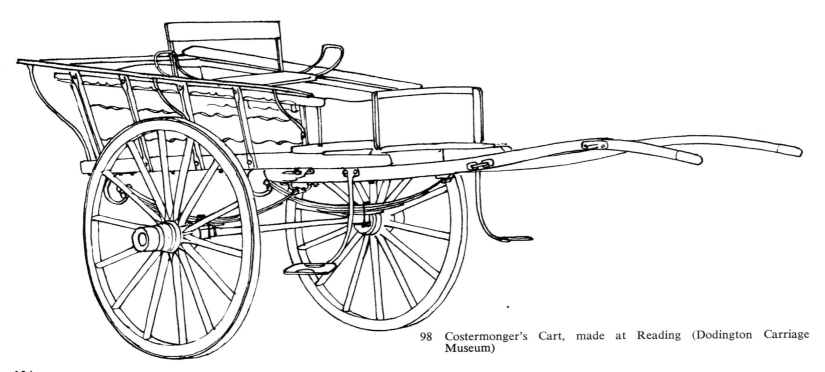

98 Costermonger's Cart, made at Reading (Dodington Carriage Museum)

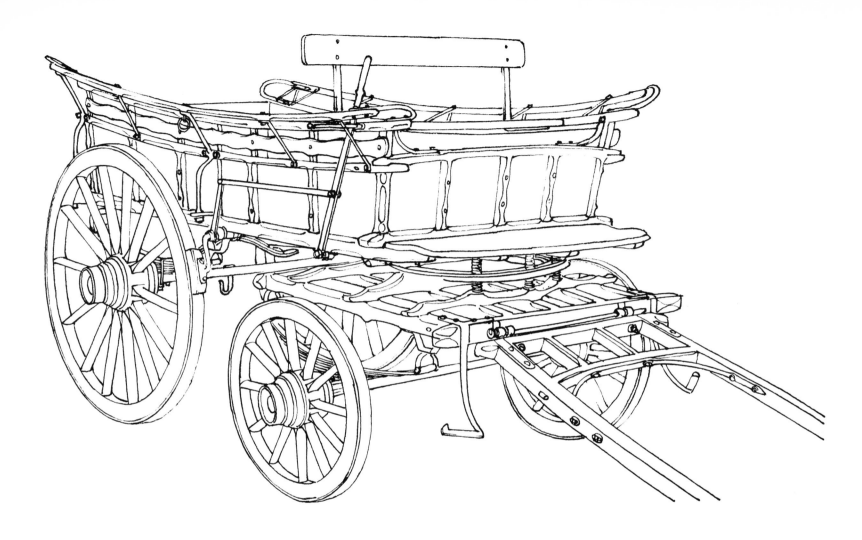

Both had mail-type straight axles and each was made in three sizes ranging from 6 to 20cwt.

The Butcher's Spring-cart, as made by Bristol, was similar to a Market Cart and showed no variation from the heavier carts that were dealt with in Chapter 4.

The Dodington Carriage Museum has a Costermonger's Cart that was built at Reading (illus 98). In terms of design and finish it is a masterpiece. The bent shafts are lap-joined below the side-pieces, to which the scroll-irons and brackets carrying the springs are attached. The wheels have $1\frac{1}{4}$-inch treads on a diameter of 43 inches and are built on Collinge axles with 14 spokes. The foot-

99 Hampshire Strawberry Cart, by Hayter of Porchester (Charles Martell)

100 Somerset Churn Cart (Charles Martell)

steps are on quarter-circle irons. The body is built on a series of wooden staves, with deeply cyma-curved iron standards at the hind-end. The footboard rises to a dashboard. The panelboards along the sides are carved and chamfered and the whole is deeper at the hind-end in the manner of all such carts and barrows. The seat is positioned to obtain a right balance on the shafts when driver and passenger are seated. Lamp-irons are fitted to each side at the fore-end of the body. The fitment of loops for kicking-straps suggests that the pony was usually of a spirited nature. This cart was finished with all natural wood varnished and would have belonged to a comparatively wealthy costermonger who may have been a Pearly King with his wife as Queen.

Charles Martell has three carts that have a rightful place in this survey. The largest, a four-wheeler, is a Spring-cart built by Hayter of Porchester, Hants (illus 99). It is called a Strawberry Cart because it was designed to carry that fruit to market. At the time of writing, 1978, it had been overhauled and repainted in crimson, and was and still is in regular use for general purposes.

It is a comparatively small cart, on a short wheelbase. The wheels are 32 and 49 inches in diameter on a 2-inch tread, with Drabbles axles and 12 spokes in fore and 14 in hind. It has a rectangular light forecarriage of waggon type with turntable rings on semi-elliptic springs fore and aft with 5 leaves in fore and 7 in hind, where there is a transverse damper above the hind-axle. The foot-steps are bolted to the short splinter-bar, which is designed to carry either a heavier or a lighter pair of shafts.

The brake is operated in the usual way by a right-hand lever. The body is 81 inches long with a footboard projecting another 12 inches. The lower part is fully panelled but the upper part is semi-open, with a symmetrically shaped panelboard between the mid- and top-raves. Straight-through out-raves project flatly, with hand-loop irons at each end, giving an overall width of 59½ inches, with an overall length at the top of 87½ inches. The driving-seat and back form a removable unit. Additional fitments are deep side-cratches and a grille-like tailboard.

Martell's second vehicle is a Somerset Churn Cart, made at Mark, near Highbridge (illus 100). Though of heavy build, it is on springs with mail axles and the well-braced shafts are fitted for

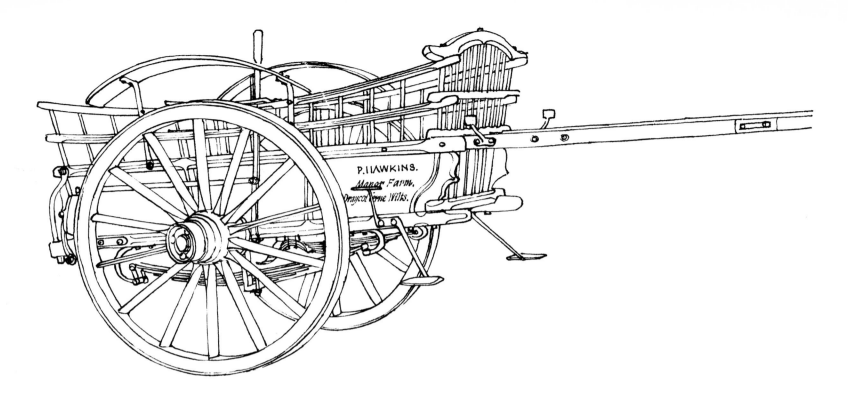

van harness. The hind axle-bed has a damper spring. The body is large and of medium depth, with the top open above the raves, with top-rails that descend to the front end. It was probably the longest type of cart to carry splashboards, indicating that the driver sat within the body. It was called a Churn Cart because there are four lengthwise strips of half-round iron screwed to the floor, along which churns could be slid with comparative ease. There are foot-steps, bolted to the shafts in front of the body. The cart was painted Oxford blue and scarlet.

The third vehicle is possibly the largest Float that I have ever seen (illus 101). The body is fully panelled with spindles all round above the floor, the lower part is closed but above the main side-pieces the body is open with middle- and top-raves. The head-rail is deeply arched and the whole ensemble is most ornate. This float is deeply cranked for large wheels, which had been removed for repair at the time I saw it. They are built on mail axles with 14 spokes and 3-inch tread. The 6 leaf-springs are hung on scroll-irons with a transverse damper. Quite wide and concentric splash-boards rise well above the side of the body. The cart is fitted with a lever-brake working inverted shoes behind the wheels. The double foot-step is well thought out, enabling driver and passenger to board the float at the fore-end with ease. The Float is in its original colours of buff and scarlet, with lamp-irons at shaft level. The Float was owned by P. Hawkins, of Manor Farm, Draycot Cerne, Wilts (between Chippenham and Christian Malford). Such a cart, without its wheels, provided an opportunity to examine the essential features of a mail axle.

The term Spring-cart was commonly applied to four-wheeled vehicles of light or medium weight, and one is much exercised to distinguish between Spring-carts and Market Carts. Both were used for market work and either could be on four wheels or two. While some were comparatively plain and simple, there were many that were sufficiently ornate to leave no doubt about their origin, which they shared with the various types of passenger cart. Many of the four-wheeled carts had a further span of working life on farms.

Their undercarriages varied considerably, so that while many had the lighter van type of carriage, there were others with a

137

102 Chiltern Corn-chandler's Cart

waggon type of carriage, with the wheels and shafts correspondingingly heavier. The latter type had no springs and with a straight and semi-open body seems to have been a hybrid between the road vehicles and farm waggons.

An example of this type was noted in 1948 at Wexham, between Uxbridge and Slough. The whole robust undercarriage could have carried a much heavier body. The heavy-draught type of shafts were draught-pinned to the forecarriage hounds. The large fore-wheels were designed for a quarter lock and, with the hind, had van-type naves, with the spoking 10 and 12 respectively. The body had iron standards and middle-raves all round and was fully closed in waggon style. It was finished in blue and red with a red undercarriage, and branded 'R. P. Grenville-Morgan Esq., Langley Park, Wexham, Bucks.'

A more ornate and conventional Spring-cart was found in the Chilterns and bore the name J. Batchelor on the headboard with no further identification (illus 102). It had a short body with straight raves and spindled sides and front. The ornamental panel-boards left the bodywork partially open in the manner typical of such carts. The rectangular forecarriage had a turntable ring, allowing a full lock. The van-type shafts were straight and hinged to a splinter-bar. The wheels had van-type naves with 12 spokes in fore and 14 in hind, on semi-elliptic springs with a transverse damper over the hind axle-bed.

In Ayrshire, a very fine 'Retail Market Cart' was made by Alexander Jack & Sons Ltd, of Maybole. In general appearance it may be said to have 'stemmed' from the farmer's Market Cart, because it could alternatively have been used as a passenger cart, seating four persons, back-to-back. The fore-part of the body was open to a dashboard and the low, boarded sides were open between the upper rails. It could carry four large churns with all their taps turned outward beyond the body at the sides and tail. No tailboard was fitted and in its place there was a wooden bar, fitting over the ends of the raves, in the manner of the waggons

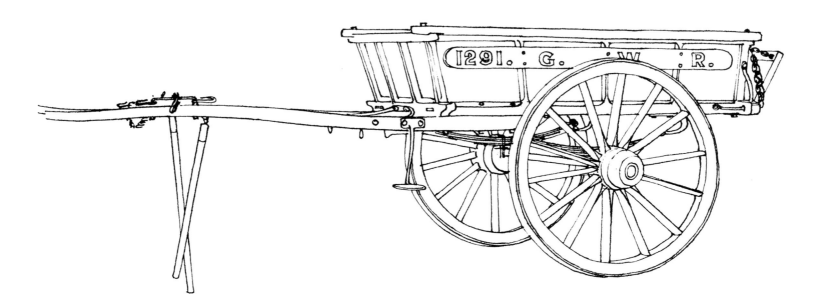

103 Light Spring-cart, by Great Western Railway at Swindon (Oxford Railway Publishing Co/British Rail)

of Kent and East Sussex. The wheels had 14 spokes on mail, straight-through axles, mounted on semi-elliptic springs. Fore and hind foot-steps were fitted to the near side and the shafts were bent for van harness.

Jack also made a range of light two-wheeled carts for various purposes, all deriving from the Ayrshire Harvest Cart shown in my book *Farm Waggons and Carts* (David & Charles). They were all quite distinctive in design and they had the type of nave peculiar to many Scottish and Irish carts, in which the linchpin was outside the face of the nave, and not within, as in English carts. There appears to have been no means of preventing the linchpin from jumping out through vibration.

A Wiltshire Traveller's Cart was briefly mentioned above and may now be treated in more detail. The example concerned was owned by a picturesque man named Hicks, who worked a considerable area that centred on Tetbury. He always wore a broad-brimmed hat and a knee-length waggoner's smock. His cart was geared for heavy draught but with a vanner in the shafts. He always had a donkey or two tethered to the tail of the cart, which was of considerable dimensions, hence the gear. The 54-inch wheels were built on mail axles with 14 spokes and the cart was mounted on semi-elliptic springs. The line of the body had that pronounced sheer, with deep removable boards, peculiar to Wiltshire Carts.

Mr Hicks was reputed to have been born about 1820 and lived a hale life into what is regarded as living memory. There must have been many such men on the road during the nineteenth century.

The patient donkey played a much larger part in country life than we may realise and all kinds of people made good use of one. We may also be surprised at the work a donkey could do. They were all geared with cart or light-van harness and such gear is still in use today. The donkey and cart was very much favoured by traders, costermongers, countrywomen and children.

A diagram from the Swindon drawing-office of the Great Western Railway, for a Light Cranked-axle Cart, was made in 1900 (illus 103). The tare and capacity are not shown, but the cart would make an interesting subject for the modeller, because of its features. The body is 22 inches deep at the fore-end and 19 inches at the hind-end, with an overall width of 48¾ inches, and a length at the floor of 94 inches. The body is equipped with a white canvas tilt and the four hoops are braced by seven rails set equidistantly.

The straight van-shafts overlap the main-sides on the inside, giving the appearance of mid-raves to the body. This has wooden spars and is supported at the hind-end by iron standards. The panelboards are nicely carved at their projecting fore-ends and the whole body is well chamfered. The tailboard has a draught-pin through both hinges, for easy removal. At the fore-end of the body there is an inverted 'tripod' stand, to take the weight with the shaft-blades clear of the ground, when the horse is not in the shafts. The 48-inch wheels have a tread of 2¾ inches and were built on Drabbles axles, with 12 spokes.

Another diagram of a Great Western Railway One-horse Float shows this fairly light vehicle fitted with heavy-draught shafts, that is with long staples and tip-sticks. This cart was not greatly dissimilar from the Cranked-axle Cart, except that it ran on wheels having a diameter of 54 inches. The diagram was dated 1889.

A year before, in 1888, Swindon produced a diagram for a tip-cart that was also geared for heavy draught. It had a tare weight of 12cwt. The shaft was hinged, the body a little in front of the axle line. The axle-bed had two sets of riser-blocks with a thin transverse piece between the two sets. The wheels appear to have been built on Collinge through axles, bolted to the axle-bed. The 54-inch wheels had a 3½-inch tread with 14 spokes staggered on wooden naves. The body was 30 inches deep at the fore-end and 22 inches at the tailboard. The sides had removable boards, each on three pegs reaching down to the floor level. They were uniformly 15½ inches deep.

The GWR also made a van-geared Parcels Van, which was dated 1887. This was a closed van, for one horse, and had a tare of 15/16cwt, to carry 15cwt. It had a light forecarriage on double elliptic springs, with 39-inch wheels, while the hind-wheels of 54 inches diameter were hung on single springs suspended on scroll-irons. The wheels were built on mail axles. A pedal-type brake operated through cranks and rods on to the hind-wheels. The body was 84 inches long by 52 inches wide at the floor and measured 52½ inches from the floor to the eaves of a flattish roof which was extended forward to provide a 24-inch canopy for the driver. There were rails all round to contain additional light parcels.

For similar work in country districts, the South Eastern Railway, before joining with the London, Chatham and Dover, used a rather larger Parcels Van, although its tare weight at 13cwt was lighter by reason of a canvas tilt. This van had twice the weight capacity of the GWR Van, at 30cwt. That it was geared for heavy draught, suggests that the dividing line between heavy and van draught was between 15 and 20cwt. The equivalent van on the GWR, dated 1889, built to a tare weight of 17cwt to carry the same load, was van-gear shafted. Although this last van was classified as a goods vehicle it was, in fact, used by the passenger department. The tilt of this GWR van was unusual in having a canopy over the driver's seat.

The contents of this book may be summarised by saying that the total number of all types and variant designs or patterns of these types is inexhaustible and to include more than has been included would require a work of the size of one volume of the *Shorter Oxford English Dictionary*. The vehicles mentioned have been chosen to provide as complete a coverage as is possible within the practicable limits of this book and the illustrations have been provided to that same end. Inevitably, there have been those omissions that might have been included, but it has been necessary in some cases to show more than one example of a type in order to indicate the remarkable diversity. One may open the Laurie & Marner catalogue for 1898 and find no less than nine patterns of Victoria. If the writer were to confine himself within the limit of one each for each type then the reader would be left with quite false conclusions.

# Index

**carriages:**
Barouche, 14, 40, 50
Berlin, 14, 36
Britzska, 39
Brougham, 25, 49-51;
  Landaulette-Brougham, 51;
  Brougham-waggonette, 53,
  54, 61
Cabriolet, 25, 36, 48, 49
Caleche, 14, 39
Chaise, 18, 46
Chariot, 36, 46, 47
Clarence, 25, 50, 52
Curricle, 36, 47, 48
Dress-chariot, 36, 37
Landau: Canoe Landau
  (Sefton), 42, 43; Dress
  Landau, 41; origin, 15, 40;
  Sociable, 42, 44; Square
  Landau (Shelborne), 41, 42;
  State coach, 38; Victoria, 43,
  45; Vis-a-vis, 38
Phaeton: Basket, 54;
  Beaufort, 55; Demi-mail, 55;
  High-perch, 47, 55; Mail, 55,
  56; origin, 54; Park, 54;
  Pony, 54; Stanhope, 57, 58;
  Village, 58
Post-chaise, 18, 46; Chariot,
  46, 47

Pomeranian, 10, 47
Break: Body, 61; definition,
  61; Shooting, 59, 60;
  Skeleton, 61
Fourgon, 62
Waggonette, 34, 60, 63;
  definition, 61; Lonsdale 61
**carts:**
Dog-cart, 88, 89, 90
Eridge, 90, 91
Manchester, 94
Market, 94, 97ff
New England types, 85
Nottingham, 100
Shandry, 94, 95
Tennis, 100
Whitechapel, 89, 99
**components of vehicles:**
axle: Collinge, 15, 16, 23, 95,
  125; crank, 94, 97; Drabbles,
  11, 16, 125; mail, 11, 16, 23,
  95
Brakes, 23, 59, 62, 96
coach fittings, 23
draught-pole, 23
lamps, 23, 38, 54, 60, 94, 119
perch, 11, 23, 37, 55
shafts, 54, 81, 90, 96, 122, 126
springs: early, 10; Cee, 11, 36;
  elliptic, 10, 30; telegraph, 23

tyres: iron, 25; rubber, 14, 44
coachbuilders, 12, 96
**driving:**
coachmen, 20
driver's uniform, 23
guard duties, 20, 23; horses,
  9, 20, 44; uniform, 20, 23
postboys, 36, 46
postilion, 36, 39
rule of the road, 36
'tigers', 48, 55
whip, use of, 36

**Gigs:**
Buggy (Eng./Amer.), 81
Dennett, 86, 88
Dowlais, 88
Governess Cart, 93, 97
Liverpool, 88
Norfolk, 88
origin, 81
Ralli-car, 91, 92
Skeleton, 85
Stanhope, 85
Tilbury, 81
'trap', 96, 97
Tub Cart, 93
Well-bottomed, 92, 93
Whisky, 81
Whitechapel, 88, 89

**Hackney carriages**, 25, 41, 50
'growler', 25
Hansom cab, 26
sedan chair, 25
**harness:**
carriage, 36
coach, 19, 36
heavy-draught, 107. 108,
  116, 119, 122
kicking-strap, 96
pickaxe, 36, 61
tandem, 36
unicorn, 36
van-draught, 107, 108
**heavy-goods vehicles:**
Brewer's dray, 102, 108, 109
coal cart, 102, 103
Conestoga Waggon, 124
fire appliances, 116, 117, 118
Miller's waggon, 103, 104, 105,
  114, 115
Mineral Water Van, 112, 113
pantechnicon, 116
railway waggons, 106, 107
timber bob, 119, 120; waggon,
  119 121
trolley, 110, 111

London, influence of, 12

McAdam, 12

omnibuses:
    Charabanc, 33, 34
    'garden-seat', 29, 30
    horses, 29
    hotel and station, 31, 32
    'knifeboard', 29, 30, 31
    Lafitte (Paris), 29
    origin, 26
    outside seating, 26, 29
    Shillibeer, 29
    tram, 27, 31
operation of coaches,
carriages:
    hiring, 18, 46

jobmasters, 44
posting, 18, 46
stage coach expenses, 20
innkeepers, 10
horses, 10, 20
liveries, 25
postmasters, 10
tools carried, 25

Pickford's 'Flying Waggons', 10

railways, impact of, 11, 12, 21
road coaches:
    Diligence, 19
    mail-coach, 12, 13, 18, 25

Park Drag, 17, 21
stage-coach, 9, 17, 19, 20, 22,
    25
road conditions, 2, 10, 12, 20

Telford, 12
tradesmen's carts and vans:
    Baker's 129
    Brewer's covered, 130
    Butcher's, 139
    Churn, 136
    Collection/Delivery, 124, 127,
        128, 140
    Corn-chandler's, 138

Costermonger's, 134
Dairy float, 132, 133
float (various), 97, 100, 116,
    126, 132, 137
Fishmonger's, 133
Fruiterer's, 134
Ice-cream, 127
London hay-cart, 124
Spring-cart, 136, 137, 139
Strawberry, 135, 136
Traveller's, 125, 139
Turnpike Act 1773, 12

wheelwrights, 12, 96